5 - 0

Zen and the Art of the Second Serve

D.B. Nap

Published by RingSleepPictures, 2025.

ZEN AND THE ART OF THE SECOND SERVE

First edition. November 16, 2025.

Written by D.B. Nap.

MY TOP FIVE

Tennis has a way of turning confident adults into nervous beginners.

We walk onto court convinced we're here to hit forehands, but somewhere between the first double fault and the second bad call, we realize we're really here to battle our own psychology.

Every player knows that moment—the flash of panic when a once-automatic motion suddenly feels foreign, or when the opponent across the net seems to be reading your mind. The game becomes a mirror, and it reflects everything you bring to it: patience, fear, ego, resilience.

I didn't write this book to tell you how to hit the ball. I wrote it because for years, I thought that was the problem. It wasn't. The turning points in my tennis life didn't come from better technique—they came from better awareness. From recognizing patterns, reading personalities, and learning that composure is a skill you can train like a topspin backhand.

The stories that follow aren't lessons in form—they're lessons in focus. Some are funny, some painful, all earned the hard way: one point, one meltdown, one revelation at a time.

If you've ever walked off court shaking your head, knowing you lost a match you should've won, you're in the right place. Because this book isn't about mastering tennis.

It's about mastering the part of you that plays it.

Here are my top five stories in this book.

1: Make Them Hit the Shot They Hate

During the club championships, we faced off against a player JP who was a level above the rest of us, he employed a serve-and-volley game, and his tall partner who stood 6'6" was the weaker of the two players. JP positioned his towering partner close to the net, a traditional formation designed to cover the court. It was a classic example of one superior player partnering with an average player while attempting to dominate the match.

However, we discovered a fatal flaw in their setup. Despite his imposing 6'6" frame, the tall partner absolutely hated hitting overheads. Once we recognized this weakness, we began lobbing every return to neutralize the advantage JP typically gained from his service games. Remarkably, the tall partner wouldn't even attempt to cover the lobs, despite having an obvious height advantage that should have made these shots routine for him. As I recall, we didn't have to do much to get the ball over his head—his reluctance to play overheads did most of the work for us.

We ended up winning a match that, on paper, we probably should have lost. But strategically, we had found the answer to the service game of the better player, and that strategic edge proved more valuable than any physical advantage he possessed.

2: The Mind Reader Moment

Playing doubles on the far court at the club, I found myself returning in the ad court when I crushed a backhand return for an outright winner it definitely won the point and sent a message. On the next serve, I knew with certainty that I wouldn't get another backhand. I was right in my prediction, but I became so excited about correctly anticipating my opponent's strategy that I over hit the shot and sent it sailing long. This marked the first time I had successfully read an opponent's psychology and made an accurate prediction about their next move.

These kinds of predictable, Pavlovian responses occur repeatedly in doubles matches. When my partner is serving and I execute a successful poach, the opponent will inevitably test the down-the-line shot on the next point. Similarly, if I manage to pass the net player with a return down the line, they typically won't attempt to poach on the following point—and sometimes they'll abandon poaching for the remainder of the match. This type of two-dimensional thinking proves remarkably predictable in doubles play.

However, this pattern tends to disappear as opponent skill level increases. The toughest opponents don't simply react to your plays—they make adjustments to your adjustments. To succeed against thinking players, you must be superior not only in your racket skills but also in your ability to read plays and identify patterns that work against increasingly sophisticated opposition.

3: Beat Them with Misery

We had a team player whose approach to tennis was defined by sheer endurance and psychological warfare. He would bring a lawn chair and umbrella to his matches for the changeovers, signaling his dedication to being out there all day if necessary. His entire identity on court was built around being a retriever—his whole game centered on the simple principle of just making the other guy give up.

While a stronger player could beat him regularly, the common refrain was that it wasn't fun to play him. The victories came at a psychological cost that many players found draining. I remember one league match where the team score had already been decided, yet he was still out there grinding away because his opponent happened to be another retriever and pusher. At one point, he actually asked his opponent if he wanted to quit, pointing out that the result wouldn't affect the team score anyway.

His strategy was transparent but effective: making the match and the time on court as miserable as possible for his opponent. It was pure psychological endurance torture. He understood that tennis isn't just about who can hit better shots—it's also about who can outlast the other person's will to continue fighting. His lawn chair and umbrella weren't just comfort items; they were props in a mental game designed to show his opponents that he had all day, and he was perfectly comfortable making them suffer through every minute of it.

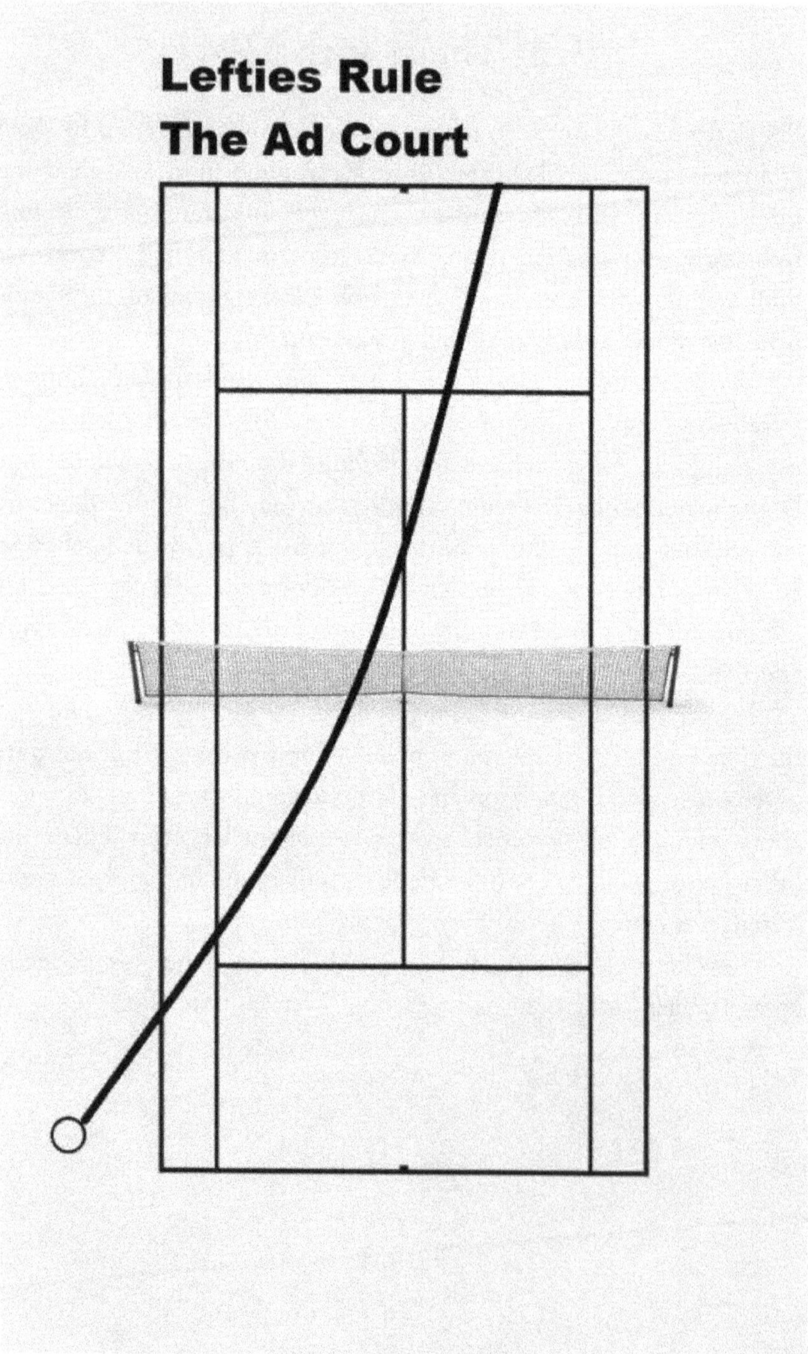
Lefties Rule
The Ad Court

4: Lefties Rule the Ad Court

The statistical advantage of left-handed players in tennis is fascinating and may help explain why lefties are disproportionately represented among tennis legends. Three of the four break points in any game occur in the ad court, giving lefties a natural edge. On these crucial points, a lefty's wide serve pulls directly into a right-hander's backhand—usually the weaker wing—providing a built-in weapon at the most pressure-filled moments.

There's also a conservative strategy paradox that surfaces on key points. When players think, *"this may be my only chance,"* they often overhit and miss. The pressure to capitalize actually leads to poor decision-making instead of better execution.

In extended rallies under pressure, both players often play not to lose rather than to win—trading safe, grinding exchanges where no one wants to take the first risk. The rally becomes a test of nerve and patience rather than bold shot-making.

I grew up playing a lefty, L.S., and what I learned from him has applied against every lefty since. (Okay, all lefties stop reading here.) Most lefties use a slice serve to exploit the ad-court angle to your backhand, so they rarely develop a high-kicking serve to that side—Nadal being the exception. My breakthrough was realizing I could expect a certain height and trajectory, not a ball jumping up above my shoulders. Once I recognized that pattern, it became about timing—waiting for the ball in that pocket and driving it down the line or crosscourt, almost like batting practice.

FLAT = ROCK, TOPSPIN = SCISSORS, NET PLAY = PAPER

5: Serve and Volley Beats Flat Hitters

I experienced a dramatic turnaround in a match that taught me one of tennis's fundamental principles. The first set was a disaster—I lost 6-0 trying to out-hit a flat ball striker, essentially playing his game. In the second set, I changed completely and won 6-1 by using kick serves and heavy topspin groundstrokes and serve and volleying and chip and charge tactics.

This revealed the net advantage: topspin creates major timing problems for flat hitters to time effectively on the return. The bouncing ball's higher trajectory and pace change force adjustments they're not comfortable making. Serve-and-volley also became effective because their flat passes lacked angles and were easy to volley.

The victory's key was flexibility. My opponent couldn't adapt because he had no other style of game to fall back on. Once I solved his style, he had no answers.

That match crystallized a universal principle—tennis has its own Rock-Paper-Scissors. Each stroke type beats another but remains vulnerable to a third. Net play beats flat shots because flat hitters can't create passing angles. Topspin beats net play by dipping the ball and opening angles. Flat shots beat topspin by taking it early and neutralizing spin's effectiveness.

History proves the pattern. Rafael Nadal's heavy spin fell to Robin Soderling's flat power at the French Open. Rod Laver's topspin revolution beat serve-and-volleyers like John Newcombe on grass, exposing their vulnerability to dipping passes. Before Laver, nearly everyone served and volleyed on grass because flat shots offered limited angles, making passes nearly impossible. The cycle repeats through tennis history—each style dominates until its counter-style inevitably appears.

MIND OVER MATCH

Tennis rewards the player who can think one shot ahead—but it crowns the one who can stay calm while doing it. Matches are rarely lost on mechanics alone. They slip away through hesitation, impatience, or the silent tug-of-war between confidence and doubt. The mind is both the coach and the opponent, offering clarity one moment and chaos the next. Master it, and the scoreboard tends to follow.

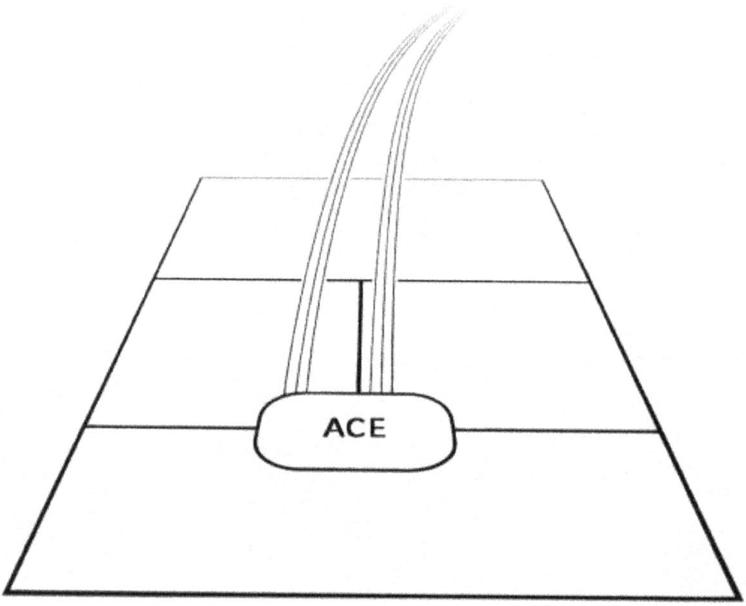
ACE

6: Confidence Is Contagious - Even to You

At my peak performance, I possessed absolute confidence in my basic slice serve, which I could hit hard and with remarkable consistency. My confidence was so complete that when I received a bad line call on my first serve, I would intentionally place the second ball in exactly the same spot, essentially daring my opponent to call both serves out.

During tough or tight moments in matches, I developed the habit of hitting two first serves. I had reached such a level of confidence and technical mastery that this approach made perfect sense to me. My reasoning was simple: given two serves aimed at the same location and the same spot, my odds of success increased dramatically. I essentially had two chances to make one serve, and I genuinely liked those odds.

My approach was so unconventional that it drew comments from opponents. One memorably opponent asked me, "You know it's a second serve, right?" But that question missed the point entirely—I knew exactly what I was doing, and the strategy worked because my technique and confidence supported it.

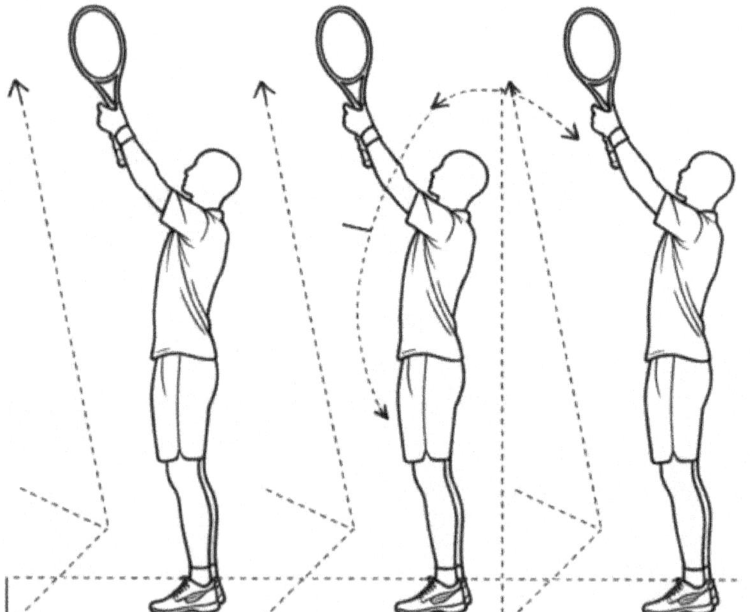

Toss drift

7: Exploit the Tell

I had a good friend who was a lefty with an impressive delivery that proved difficult to handle in most situations. However, I eventually discovered a slight tell in his service motion: his toss would wander slightly, revealing his directional intent before he made contact with the ball. Once I picked up on this pattern, I could level the playing field and handle his service games with much more neutrality.

One day I decided to tell him about what I'd noticed. He immediately denied that his toss varied and proceeded to demonstrate what he called his "universal toss," showing me that he could hit any spot from the same ball placement. Perhaps when he was mentally focused and consciously thinking about his technique, he could maintain consistency in his toss. But during actual match conditions, when he wasn't actively monitoring this aspect of his serve, his tell continued to show up. The difference between his controlled demonstration and his automatic match play revealed the gap between conscious technique and ingrained patterns under pressure.

THAT WAS OUT, BUI'L GIVE IT TO YOU.

8: The Gamesmanship Story

In most matches, I assumed I'd receive at least two or three bad line calls—it was simply human nature. What mattered was recognizing how and when they happened. Some players just can't help themselves; if the ball lands near the line, they call it out. Once I spotted that pattern, I mentally shrank the part of the court they were hitting into by the same distance they were stealing from me—an eye-for-an-eye method of restoring fairness.

I developed what I called an escalation protocol for handling bad calls. After the first questionable one, I'd ask "Are you sure?" and move on. If it happened again, I'd repeat the question but hold my gaze longer—sending the message: *I know what you're doing, and now you know that I know.* For most reasonable players, that subtle warning ended the issue.

I also used what I called the preemptive strike. Early in the match, I'd make an obvious bad call in their favor—deliberately playing a ball that was clearly out. It established me as an honest player, maybe even too honest. Later, when a close call went my way, it looked like an honest miss, not a cheat balancing the scales.

Strategic timing completed the approach. If my opponent made a bad call at thirty-all, mine would come on break point. We might both bend the rules, but I made sure my version served a tactical purpose, not just retaliation.

9: Fake Calm, Real Confidence

I found myself in the uncomfortable position of being the weakest player on court—my partner was stronger, and both opponents were stronger as well. I could play at this level, but only at peak performance; anything less got me in trouble quickly.

This created what I called the coverage dilemma. On shots falling between us, I constantly calculated: do I take it or let my partner? I knew he could handle it better, but if I didn't take my share, he'd end up covering sixty to seventy percent of the court, turning it into mixed doubles. That wasn't fair to him, and it wasn't my role to shrink from responsibility.

There was also the target psychology you can't ignore. Deep down, you know when both opponents have a choice, the next ball is coming to you. You have to stand up and take it, or you'll just keep seeing more and more balls. It's a bad feeling—looking around for help while not wanting to admit you need it.

Instead of retreating and forcing my partner to play a mixed-doubles match against two men, I decided I was better off taking my shots and living with the results. The logic was simple: play timidly and you may not be asked back. Everyone wants to play up to test themselves, but you also need to play down sometimes to even things out. It's tennis karma—you earn your place in the rotation by showing up and competing, even when overmatched.

10: Weather the Storm Together

I was playing a college match at home in doubles, during the last matches of the day. Our match was close and competitive when it started to sprinkle. We kept playing, and remarkably, no one even said a word about stopping. Then it started raining harder, and still we continued—again, no one said a word.

At that moment, I realized what was happening. Neither team wanted to reschedule this match. Everyone on court wanted this result to be final, no matter what conditions we had to endure to get there. By the end, we were playing in a downpour, and the quality of tennis had declined as you'd expect when the court is soaked and visibility is poor. The match ultimately concluded when a net cord fell on our side of the net for the winning shot.

Everyone got their wish—we didn't have to play again or see them again. It was an unspoken psychological agreement among all four players to finish the match no matter what the conditions became. Sometimes the desire to have closure and finality outweighs any concern about playing conditions or the quality of play. We all understood this without needing to articulate it, and we all silently committed to seeing it through to the end, rain be damned.

11: The Fake Injury Specialist

I was playing in a mixed combo league with a ringer female partner—a decent player who had some rust but no prior rating in the system. Our opponents included a college guy who arrived at the courts moaning about having had a terrible night. He complained about drinking too much or partying too hard, and he looked like he was just dragging himself to the bleachers to fulfill his obligation.

Watching him, I genuinely thought he might quit mid-match. I actually felt bad for the guy, seeing him in such apparent distress. But when the match started, it was like someone flipped a switch—the light went on and suddenly he was racing for shots, running all over the court, and even covering his female partner's shots with energy and athleticism. Then, back at the changeover, he'd revert to his suffering act: "Oh guys, I don't know if I'm gonna make it."

I was absolutely furious because I had genuinely felt bad for him originally, right up until I saw that he was sandbagging. We ended up losing a match we should have won. The frustrating part was that we probably would have played differently—with more intensity and focus from the start—if we hadn't been deceived by his fake gamesmanship. He'd manipulated our psychology before the first ball was even struck, and by the time we realized what was happening, we were already behind and playing catch-up mentally.

nice serve!

12: Ignore Backhanded Compliments

I ran into this tactic a couple of times during my playing career. Opponents would offer compliments about my forehand or second serve during changeovers, sometimes even going so far as to say something like, "I like how you keep your racket down too long but recover."

The comments were something subtle but just enough to plant a seed in the back of your mind every time you hit that shot again. The remarks were usually subtle enough that you couldn't tell for sure if they were being genuine or trying to mess with your head. Were they actually admiring my technique, or were they trying to make me overthink a shot that had been working automatically?

This tactic generally didn't work on me, but the fact that I encountered it multiple times from different opponents told me it was a recognized form of psychological warfare. It was gamesmanship disguised as friendly coaching advice—a way to introduce conscious thought into what should be an unconscious, grooved stroke. The brilliance of it was the plausible deniability. If you called them out on it, they could act offended that you'd misinterpreted their genuine compliment. But the damage might already be done, with you now thinking about mechanics in the middle of a match instead of just playing.

13: Handle Drama, Don't Create It

My wife was playing women's doubles on a court with a visible tear in the net near the top, close to the strap. During a point, a shot went straight through the hole, but because it was so close to the top, it looked like a let cord—the ball seemed to clip the net on its way over.

Then the arguing began. The opponents claimed it was a let in their favor, while our team insisted the ball had gone through the hole and the point was ours. Witnesses and teammates all weighed in, but nothing was ever settled. I think the other team just took the point—and probably the match—because I remember plenty of discussion afterward, the kind that doesn't happen when you've won and moved on satisfied.

The only memorable part of that match turned out to be an unfortunate call caused by a minor equipment failure. In situations like that, there's rarely a true resolution—only the question of who will back down or act more magnanimously. Sadly, incidents like these aren't rare at the club level and probably drive players away from the game more than anything else.

It's too bad that *The Code*—the USTA's guide to fair play and unwritten rules—wasn't applied here, which is exactly why it exists. But in competitive women's league matches, fair play often goes out the window, and what should be a sporting resolution becomes a battle of wills instead.

14: Friends Today, Enemies at Match Point

There's a famous professional match between an aging player and a younger journeyman. Before the match, they were genuine friends off court—they went fishing together and hung out like normal friends, with a relationship extending well beyond tennis.

After the match, which the older player won, he completely ghosted the younger one—never called or returned calls, and the friendship was over. The irony is striking: the veteran won, which reveals his mentality. It would make more sense if the younger player had won and the older man felt bitter about losing to someone he'd mentored. But it was the opposite—the winner severed the friendship.

The veteran approached matches like boxing bouts, turning opponents into enemies. This time, he made a friend into one, sacrificing their bond to his competitive mindset. A later documentary exposed this psychological brutality and the dark side of his drive.

Ironically, I experienced something similar. My partner and I often crossed paths with two regular opponents—a tall guy with an easy, powerful serve and his scrappy red-haired partner who fought for every point. Early on, they usually beat us, and both were cordial, chatting before matches whether we faced them or others.

Then we finally beat them. The big guy stayed friendly, but the redhead never spoke to us again. The shift was immediate and complete, as if our victory were a personal betrayal rather than just competition's natural outcome.

LUCK
LUCK
? ! ?
!!?

15: Use a Mental Timeout

I was playing a league match against a seasonal opponent with a big, loopy forehand whip shot he loved to hit. I knew it was coming every time but still struggled to handle it. Combined with his home-court advantage—knowledge of wind and slope—he was nearly unbeatable there.

I was finally getting the better of him when he took a bathroom break. My teammate reported he was puking his guts out, so we might actually win. We did, but the victory felt hollow. I'd wanted to beat him at his best since he'd beaten me so often before.

Later I realized he didn't have much beyond that forehand but could hide his weaker shots by always playing the deuce side in doubles. His bathroom break became psychological warfare against himself—his body betrayed him, not his opponent.

Something similar happened in a local tournament final. The tall guy from that same team had a new partner, and my partner and I finally met them in the championship we'd chased for years. They were spent from their semifinal and just going through the motions. We won easily, but the title still felt hollow.

All those other years when we'd fought harder and played better, we came up short. Yet this time, everything fell our way, and the ease dulled the sweetness of victory. That's tennis: sometimes you just have to show up, and other times, when you think you should win, you don't. The tennis gods are fickle, handing out favors with no regard for who deserves them most.

PATTERNS & PRESSURE POINTS

Every player has patterns—habits hidden in plain sight. The serve they trust at deuce, the rally they run under stress, the shot they abandon when nerves rise. Pressure doesn't invent weakness; it exposes it. Learning to read those patterns—and rewrite your own—is how good players turn into problem-solvers.

16: Lob Until They Learn

We were playing a night match at North Dallas Tennis Club when I discovered that my opponent couldn't hit overheads due to the strange lighting setup. The lights were pointed downward, and when lobs went above the light level, the ball would disappear temporarily before reappearing on its descent. This created a huge blind spot that made overhead smashes nearly impossible to execute.

The perfect tactical solution was glaringly obvious: lob every point to win the match. It was a clear path to victory, handed to me by the quirks of the facility's lighting design. But we lost the match because social norms prevented us from executing the strategy. It would have looked too strange to lob every single point, and we couldn't bring ourselves to do something that felt so outside the boundaries of how tennis is "supposed" to be played, even though it was completely legal and tactically sound.

The insight from this match stayed with me: sometimes the perfect tactical solution conflicts with social tennis expectations. There's an unwritten code about how matches should look and feel, and violating that code—even when it would guarantee victory—carries a psychological cost. I couldn't overcome my own sense of what was acceptable, and my opponent's weakness remained unexploited. I left the court having learned that knowing the right strategy and being willing to execute it are two entirely different things.

BODY
SEVE
BODY
SEVE
BODY
SEVE
BODY
SRVE

17: Pre-Position Your Return

One match there was an opponent who served everything directly into the body—he never varied his placement to the corners. The pattern was strange, but it proved both effective and remarkably consistent. Most players try to mix up their serve placement to keep returners off balance, but he had found something that worked for him and stuck with it religiously.

My solution came through experimentation: I began pre-positioning by sliding to one side before or during my return. Once I started doing this, I could handle his serves neutrally, turning what had been an advantage for him into routine rallies. By anticipating his single pattern, I eliminated the element that made it effective—the jam factor of hitting right at my body.

The insight from this match was clear: some players find one successful strategy and ride it exclusively, but in doing so they become completely predictable. What works brilliantly against unprepared opponents becomes a liability once someone recognizes the pattern and adjusts. His unwillingness or inability to vary his serve placement meant that once I solved the puzzle, he had no Plan B to fall back on. Consistency without variation can be a strength up to a point, but it also creates a ceiling on effectiveness against observant opponents.

NEW GEOMETRY 101

18: Respect Tennis Geometry

This was a history lesson from Allen Fox about the evolution of tennis strategy. When three of the four Grand Slams were played on grass, serve-and-volley tactics ruled. The fast, low-bouncing surfaces favored players who could reach the net quickly and finish points with volleys.

The game changer came with Rod Laver's use of topspin on both wings, which dramatically expanded the angles for passing shots. Topspin let the ball dip sharply within the lines, fundamentally changing the geometry of the game. Net rushers now faced passes that cleared the net high yet still landed in, creating angles once considered impossible or too risky.

The final blow to serve-and-volley dominance came later with polyester strings. These produced massive spin and allowed players to hit extreme angles from anywhere on court. Heavy topspin became routine, even on defense, leaving net players few safe targets.

The result was a total transformation of professional tennis. Serve-and-volley went from dominant to nearly obsolete. The blend of Laver's innovation and the rise of polyester strings proved that tennis evolution isn't just about skill—it's about how technique and technology continually redefine what strategies work.

WARM-UP

19: Scout in the Warm-Up

My method during warm-up was to test opponents with different shots while studying their serve practice patterns, gathering intelligence before the match officially began. But I've heard the common oversight that plagues non-observant players: Statements like they didn't even notice an opponent was left-handed until they actually started playing points. It's embarrassing how tunnel-vision can make you miss something so fundamental.

One key tell I learned to watch for was overhead practice. Do they take any overheads during warm-up? Are they solid and confident, or do they look uncomfortable? This single observation could determine my entire tactical approach for the match.

One specific opponent who hit every warm-up overhead as hard as humanly possible. He even tagged me with one during the pre-match routine. This was a lower-skilled player who genuinely believed that hitting everything hard could level the playing field against more technically proficient opponents. His aggression during warm-up was clearly intentional—a statement that he wouldn't be intimidated.

My immediate response was a revenge mentality. I spent the entire match looking for payback, waiting for the perfect opportunity to return the favor with a crushing overhead of my own. But I never got a sitter—never received the easy put-away opportunity I was hoping for. The irony wasn't lost on me: my focus on revenge probably distracted me from playing my best tactical tennis, which was exactly what his aggressive warm-up had been designed to accomplish.

20: Play With the Wind, Not Against It

The perfect setup occurred one day at the city courts in breezy conditions. I served with the wind at my back, my lefty partner in the opposite direction—and crucially, neither of us ever had to serve into the sun. It was an ideal alignment that gave us a huge advantage.

The result was dominant: we were winning service games at love, with our opponents barely touching returns. They grew so frustrated they accused me of being "semi-professional," unable to believe recreational players could handle them so easily.

The truth was it had nothing to do with superior skill—it was pure environmental advantage. We'd won the lottery on court assignment and spin of the racket, and we exploited it completely.

That match taught me several tactical lessons about wind. Lobbing with it becomes a weapon, and overheads are easier with it behind you since it holds the ball up longer. I'd always hated windy matches until that first wind-aided win. Then I realized the key: I only had to handle the wind better than my opponent, not beat it outright.

Over time, I developed wind tactics—extra steps for positioning, firmer volleys, tighter focus, even pausing between serves to wait for lulls. Players from Florida, raised in constant wind, stayed calm while I still had to think through each adjustment.

The lesson was humbling: wind doesn't just test your strokes; it exposes how solid your entire game really is

21: Sun and Shadows Change the Game

The sun's schedule creates predictable problems depending on when you play. An 11am start typically creates difficulties for righties, while a 2pm match puts lefties at a disadvantage when serving from certain ends. The basic strategy was simple: hope the sun moves enough after a few games of serving from each side so you could actually see your toss.

I tried various equipment solutions over the years. Caps and sunglasses helped slightly, providing some relief in marginal conditions. But when you had direct sun positioned right behind your toss, none of it mattered—you were going to see spots regardless of what you wore. The bright disc of the sun would burn into your retinas for those crucial split seconds when you needed to track the ball.

The reality was inescapable: you're seeing spots for a few seconds no matter what protective measures you take. It wasn't a problem you could solve, only one you could manage. The key became learning to serve effectively even when you couldn't see clearly, relying on muscle memory and routine rather than visual tracking. Some days you just had to accept that half your service games would be compromised by nature itself, and the match would be decided by who could handle that disadvantage with more composure.

It was usually not as bad on one side as the other. The sun might be impossible on the deuce court but not as bad on the ad or vice versa. So you just have to manage those conditions, use your normal gameplan and serve where the sun allows and make whatever compensation on the impossible side to just get the ball in play.

22: Trust the First-Set Vibe

This awareness emerged during what I think of as my pre-awakening era, before I had developed any real court strategy consciousness. I began noticing a pattern: I could sense the win or loss outcome after just the first few games of a match.

It's important to make some distinctions about what this feeling represented. It wasn't a self-fulfilling prophecy—I still tried my hardest regardless of what I sensed. And it wasn't about giving up or losing motivation. Rather, it was about sensing the trajectory of the match based on how things were unfolding. There was a certain vibe to each match: things were either working or they weren't, and that general state tended to hold for the entire duration.

The match reality I observed was that there were very few comebacks or dramatic momentum swings. Both players typically stuck to their games, and whoever had the advantage early usually maintained it. The patterns established in those opening games proved remarkably persistent.

Looking back, I recognize this as sort of the sunrise of me becoming awake on court—but it was just the beginning. I had developed the ability to read what was happening, to sense the flow and likely outcome. But I was still limited by a crucial gap: I could predict the trajectory, but I didn't yet know what to DO with that information. I could see the storm coming but had no idea how to change course or adjust my sails. That understanding would come later, but this early pattern recognition was the first crack of light breaking through.

23: Match Strategy to Opponent Archetype

Observing two players matchup perfectly illustrates how one-dimensional strategy can create extreme vulnerability. Player one was AC, a righty who ran around his backhand at all costs. Player two was EW, a lefty who became AC's perfect nemesis.

The pattern was clear: AC avoided backhands like the plague, building his entire game around hitting forehands. Against most opponents this worked, but the flaw appeared against left-handers. A lefty's natural slice serve in the ad court targets a right-hander's backhand, and for AC—who had systematically neglected that wing—it was devastating.

The results spoke for themselves. AC beat most players in his peer group but lost badly to EW almost every time. The matchup wasn't even competitive; their styles predetermined the outcome.

AC's problem wasn't pressure choking—it was a flawed game plan. He'd committed so completely to his forehand that when he met an opponent whose natural game exploited his weakness, he had no Plan B. His avoidance had become so ingrained he couldn't adapt even when the situation demanded it.

The lesson was clear: no matter how polished, a one-dimensional strategy creates vulnerability to the right opponent. AC's forehand was excellent, but his refusal to develop a reliable backhand ensured certain players would always have his number.

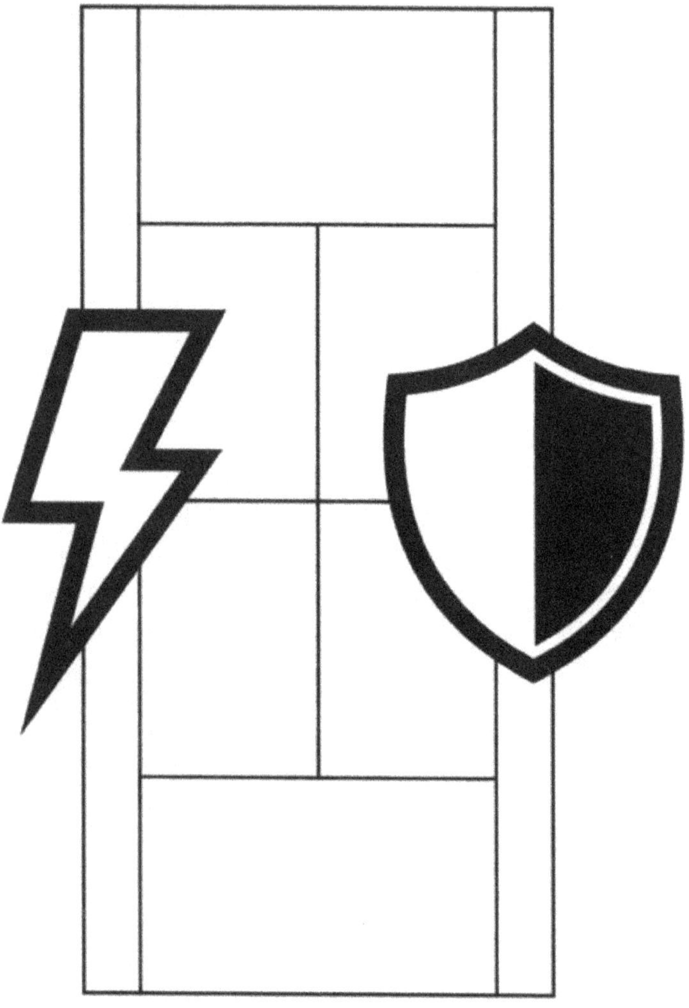

24: Deuce is for Risk, Ad is for Safety

Everyone struggle with those long, grinding games—the kind that went deuce, ad, deuce, ad in an endless stalemate where neither player could break through. I asked teaching pros and fellow players for advice on how to handle these situations, but the no one had a real solution to offer.

Eventually, I developed my own approach based on a simple philosophy that differentiated between the two score situations. On deuce points, I played aggressively and went for my shots. The reasoning was straightforward: I could afford to lose these points because I'd still get another chance to defend. But on ad points—whether in my favor or not—I switched to conservative, percentage tennis. I would force my opponent to be the one to win the point outright rather than gifting it to them with an unforced error.

This approach became a form of psychological warfare centered on mental fatigue. The question became: who could outlast the other and gain the strategic advantage? These marathon games weren't just physically exhausting; they were mentally draining. Eventually, there would come a breaking point when opponents would abandon their patience and finally go for it, hoping that luck would be on their side. They'd try to end the agony with one big shot, and more often than not, that's when I'd win the game.

The insight I gained was that tennis wasn't always about X's and O's—the tactical diagrams and strategic positioning. Sometimes it was simply about who was willing to give more and stay out there longer, grinding through the discomfort until the other person blinked.

25: Hide and Bait on the Return

Return positioning operates on three levels of sophistication, each building on the last.

Level one: basic geometry. Divide the server's angle range—from widest serve to farthest line—and bisect it, standing midway. You might shade slightly toward your weaker wing for coverage, but the idea is simple: position yourself where you can reach the most serves.

Level two: strategic baiting. Instead of standing neutral, you deliberately give up space where you actually want them to serve, tempting the server into hitting to your preferred return side. This demands confidence in your stronger wing and a willingness to gamble they'll take the bait.

Level three: advanced deception. You show one position to influence their aim, then shift during the toss when they can't see you. This gets you into ideal position for the return you want, having already steered their serve with your stance.

At the club level, this hierarchy becomes obvious. Players hiding weak backhands stand far to one side, leaving only a sliver of court to hit into. They're effectively inviting serves to their strength, sacrificing geometry to avoid using a liability.

3040

26: Know the 30-40 Cliff

I learned this from a calculation in "The Physics of Tennis" book, and it fundamentally changed how I thought about scoring. The key finding was that 30-40 on serve equals the most statistically important point in tennis—more pivotal than any other single score situation.

The mathematical logic is straightforward: getting from 30-40 to deuce dramatically changes the odds in the server's favor for holding serve. The probability shift at this moment is larger than at any other transition point in the game. You're not just saving one game point; you're fundamentally altering the statistical landscape of the entire game.

The psychological impact mirrors the mathematics. You go from being about to lose the game—one point away from disaster—to a situation where the odds suddenly shift in your favor. The momentum and pressure completely reverse in a single point. What was almost certain defeat becomes a likely hold.

This represents the cliff-edge moment where mathematics meets psychology. It's not just that the numbers say this point matters most; players can feel it. The weight of 30-40 hangs differently than other break points because both players intuitively understand, even without knowing the statistics, that getting to deuce changes everything. The server who saves that point doesn't just survive—they reclaim control. And the returner who fails to convert that opportunity doesn't just miss one break point—they watch their statistical advantage evaporate entirely.

27: Conserve Energy Where Appropriate

Sampras was a master at conserving energy. His strategy was to essentially coast during return games, staying in points without expending maximum effort, until a genuine break opportunity appeared on the scoreboard.

The body language tell was unmistakable: his whole demeanor would change at 15-30 or 0-30. Suddenly he'd lock in with visible intensity, his movements sharper and more purposeful. He understood his own game well enough to know he would hold his serve consistently, which meant he only needed to secure one break per set to win. Why waste energy on return games at 15-0 or 30-15 when those situations rarely led anywhere?

He also taught me something important about the psychology of serving out matches or sets. It's not just about the server's nerves. But there's an equally powerful factor on the other side of the net: the returner's "last stand" mentality. When someone is facing elimination or the loss of a set, they tap into a different level of focus and aggression.

The insight is that the returner actually becomes more aggressive and inspired when facing elimination. It's their final opportunity, and that desperation creates a dangerous opponent. They have nothing to lose, so they start going for shots they wouldn't attempt earlier in the match. This mental shift can catch servers off-guard, especially if they're already dealing with their own anxiety about closing things out. The combination of server nerves and returner desperation makes serving out anything one of the most psychologically complex situations in tennis.

ATTACK
BACKHAND
SERVE TO
FOREHAND

28: Attack the Forehand Under Pressure

Modern analytics have revealed a finding that overturns traditional tennis wisdom: serving to the forehand is actually more effective than the old strategy of attacking the backhand. This discovery contradicts decades of accepted thinking. At least at the pro level.

The reasoning lies in how the game has evolved. The modern two-handed backhand has become too reliable and compact. Players have mastered it so completely that it's no longer the weakness it once was. Its short swing path and the stability of two hands make it dependable even under pressure.

The forehand, by contrast, hides a surprising vulnerability despite being most players' stronger wing. It has more moving parts—a longer swing, more rotation, greater reliance on timing and footwork. Those mechanical complexities make mid-swing adjustments difficult when a serve comes fast or off-angle.

Pressure amplifies the difference. When nerves hit on big points, compact strokes hold up better. The two-handed backhand remains solid, while the forehand—with its wider motion and tighter timing demands—breaks down more easily.

This marks a strategic shift born of data. What generations of players and coaches took as gospel—attack the backhand on the serve, especially under pressure—has been overturned by evidence. The data doesn't lie, even when it contradicts instinct.

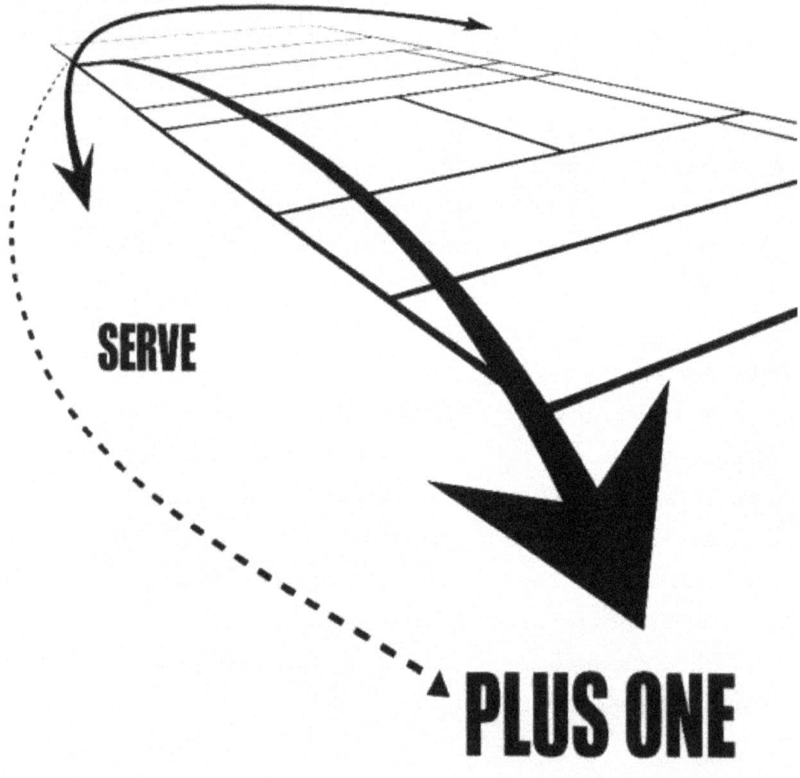
SERVE
PLUS ONE

29: Serve Plus One

Modern tennis strategy has evolved away from the traditional serve-and-volley model of winning points directly off the serve. Instead, the contemporary approach is to use the serve to set up a crushing forehand on the next shot. The serve becomes less about an ace or forcing a weak return, and more about creating the positional geometry for what comes next.

This shift has changed court positioning fundamentally. Both players now edge left of center during baseline rallies specifically to enable the inside-out forehand. This positioning has become so standard that it's created a new battleground—both players are fighting for the same real estate, trying to claim the court position that allows them to unleash their primary weapon.

The target pattern that emerged is brutally effective: hitting the inside-out forehand to the opponent's backhand combines maximum power with attacking the opponent's traditional weakness. Even though the two-handed backhand has improved dramatically, it still can't match the raw pace and heaviness that modern forehands generate, especially when hit from an open stance with full rotation.

The inside-out forehand has essentially become the money shot of modern tennis—the stroke that players build their entire tactical approach around, the shot they're trying to set up from the very first ball of every rally.

PACE

30: Use Pace as Defense

The classic tennis setup involves hitting a wide serve that pulls the returner off the court, which then opens up a sharp angle for the server's next shot. This one-two punch has been a fundamental pattern in tennis for generations—create width, then exploit the open court.

However, there's a pace constraint principle that fundamentally alters this geometry. When a returner hits a hard, aggressive return, they actually eliminate the server's extreme angle options on the next ball. The geometric reality is simple: you can't safely change direction when the incoming ball carries significant pace. The physics and biomechanics don't allow for extreme redirection of a ball that's already traveling with substantial velocity—attempting to do so dramatically increases the risk of errors or floating the ball, giving the returner time to recover.

This means the hard return functions as a defensive weapon. The returner is using pace itself to neutralize the server's angle geometry and geometric advantages. By taking time away and adding velocity, they're limiting what the server can do with their supposedly advantageous position, even when the serve has successfully pulled them wide.

The strategic insight here is that pace operates on two levels simultaneously: it creates offensive opportunities when you're the one generating it from a neutral position, but it also creates defensive constraints when you're the one trying to handle it. Speed isn't just about overpowering an opponent—it's about controlling the geometric possibilities available on the next shot. Understanding this dual nature of pace separates tactical thinkers from players who simply try to hit hard without considering the positional chess game that follows.

31: Go Bigger on the Serve

Against a good friend I was trapped in a frustrating pattern during a match—a complete break-fest where neither player could hold serve. The constant back-and-forth was maddening, and there was no rhythm or momentum building for either of us.

In my emotional response to this frustration, I started taking it out on my serve, going for significantly more pace than I had been using. It was almost born of anger rather than strategy—I was fed up with the pattern and just started ripping my serves harder.

The unexpected result caught me completely off guard: I suddenly started holding my service games while continuing to break my opponent. The shift was immediate and dramatic. This led to an aha moment that changed my approach going forward: maybe I need to go for more on my serve in general, not just when I'm frustrated.

The strategic principle that emerged was clear: you need an effective enough serve to control points and establish some baseline level of dominance in your service games. If your serve isn't creating any advantage whatsoever, you're essentially starting every point from a neutral or even disadvantageous position. The serve is supposed to be a weapon, or at minimum a way to tilt the odds in your favor.

The lesson proved to be broader than just that one match: sometimes aggression is the answer to a tactical stalemate. Increasing your offensive output—even at the risk of more errors—can break the deadlock. Calculated aggression can shift the entire dynamic of a match.

32: Depth Neutralizes Speed

An opponent named CG who was very fit and often seen running on the treadmill had seemingly endless stamina. His fitness level was off the charts, and he could run down almost anything on the court.

My initial strategy was a failed drop shot campaign. I kept trying to use finesse to beat his speed, attempting drop shots throughout the match. But I won only one out of ten attempts. The speed reality was undeniable—he was simply too fast and got to every drop shot I tried, often turning my clever tactics into easy putaways for him.

Then the breakthrough discovery: deep baseline shots could neutralize his movement advantage entirely. If I kept the ball deep and made him hit from behind the baseline, his superior speed became irrelevant. He couldn't use his legs to run down balls because there was nowhere to run—he was already backed up as far as he could go.

The tactical shift was profound—I went from trying to out-run the runner with drop shots and angles to eliminating his advantage altogether by taking away the court geometry that made his speed valuable. The result validated this approach dramatically. The set that had been shaping up as an hour-long marathon suddenly became a quick dismissal. CG was so demoralized by the change in tactics that he declined to play a second set.

The universal principle became clear: don't compete with your opponent's strength—neutralize it. I couldn't beat CG by making him run because that was his best attribute. But I could beat him by making his running ability irrelevant.

GEAR THAT WINS

Equipment doesn't win matches—but it decides how confidently you play them. The right racket, strings, and shoes erase distractions so your mind can stay where it belongs—on the next point. Every detail matters, because small comforts become big advantages when the score tightens.

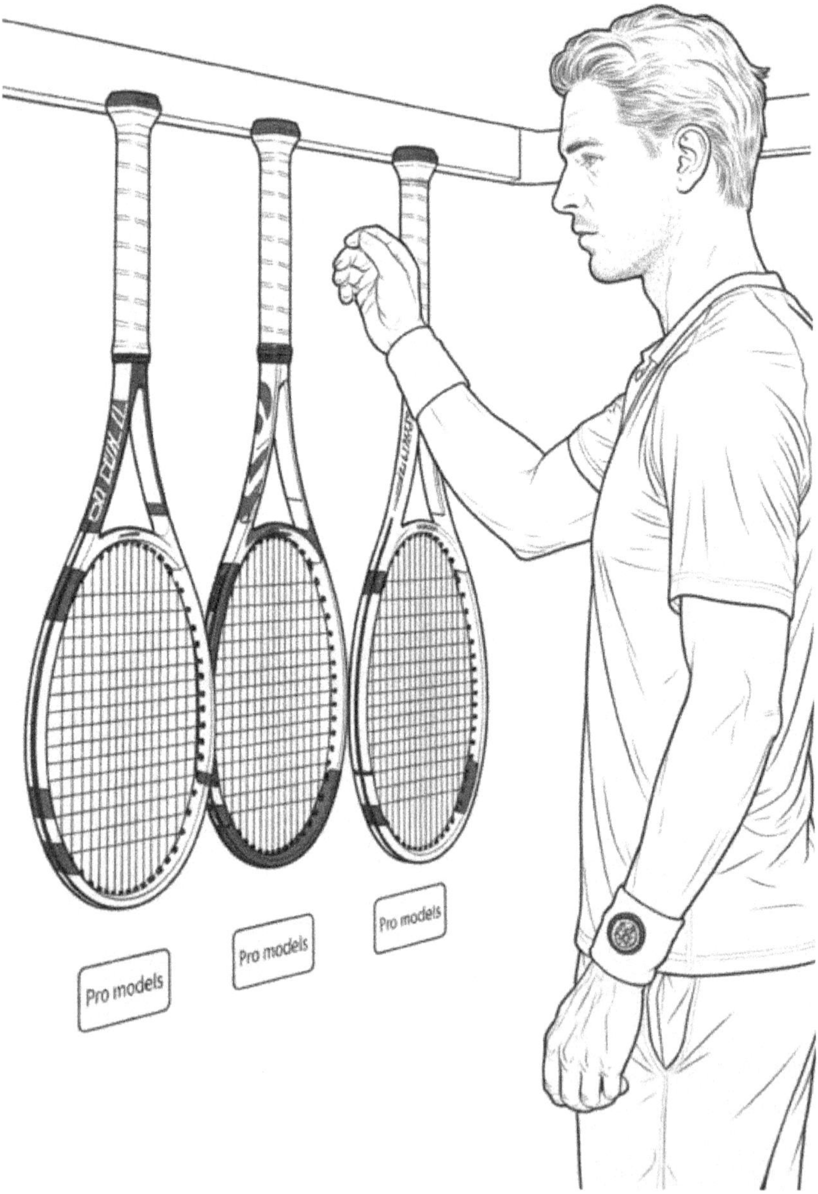
Pro models
Pro models
Pro models

33: Take it from the Pros

I hated having to switch rackets when manufacturers discontinued my model. The replacement never felt the same, and I'd go through an uncomfortable adjustment period searching for something that could replicate the performance I'd grown accustomed to. After going through this frustrating cycle enough times, I decided to change my strategy entirely.

I gave in to the choice to use rackets that main professionals were playing with. My theory was straightforward: manufacturers can't discontinue a racket that a high-level pro is actively using on tour. The professional players anchor the product line for years because the company has invested in that endorsement relationship and wants to maintain the marketing value. By following the pros' equipment choices, I was essentially buying myself time and consistency. I could be confident that replacement frames and strings would remain available, and that the model wouldn't suddenly vanish from the market just as I'd finally dialed in my game with it.

This approach wasn't about believing I needed the exact same racket as a tour player to improve my game—it was pure practicality. I was using the professionals as insurance against obsolescence, leveraging their market influence to ensure my own equipment stability. It was one less variable to worry about in a game that already had enough of them.

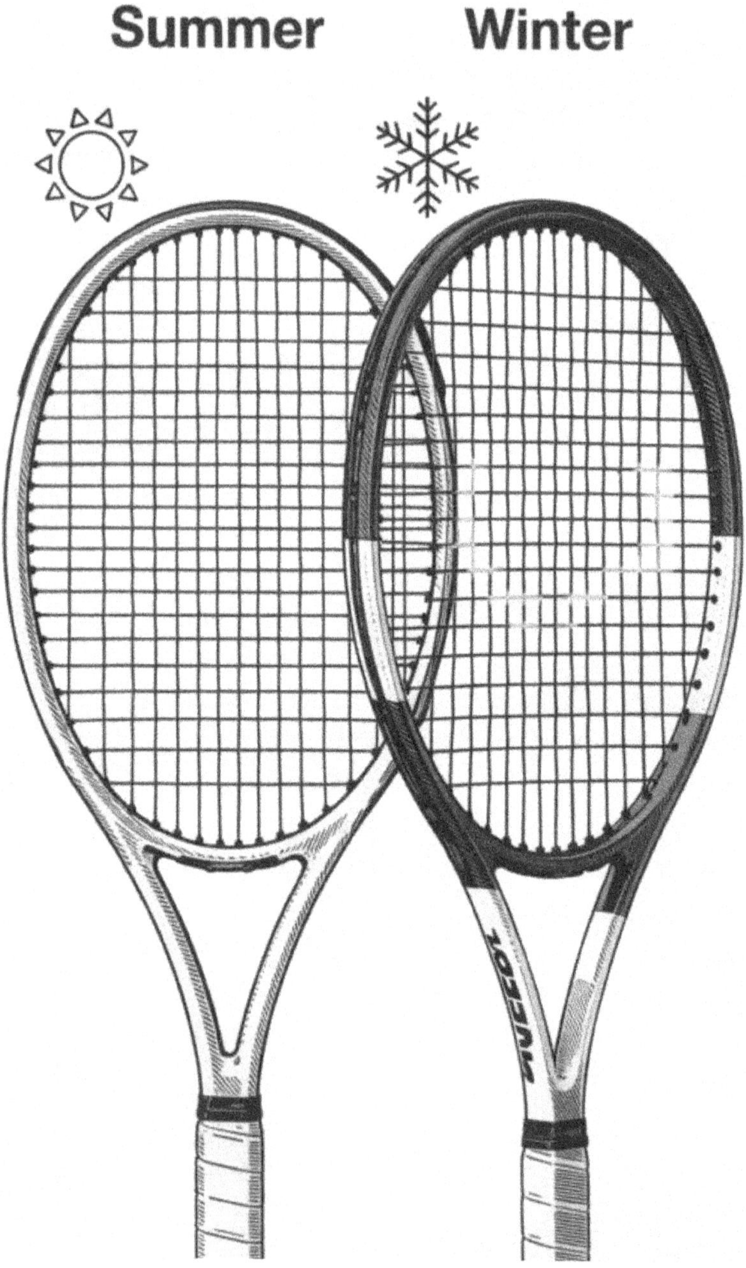
Summer
Winter

34: Adjust Tension for Temperature

My favorite string used to be Gamma Rough, which had a rubbery texture that performed beautifully in mild or cold temperatures. The string gave me excellent control and feel under normal conditions, and I'd grown to trust it completely.

But on one extremely hot day, the strings became too rubbery and loose from the heat. The tension had essentially evaporated, and the stringbed felt like a trampoline. I couldn't control the ball even during warmup—shots that should have been routine were flying unpredictably, and I had no confidence hitting any shot. It was a helpless feeling, knowing that my equipment had betrayed me before the match even started.

The learning from this experience was clear: I should have been carrying different rackets with different strings and tensions in my bag to account for varying conditions. Back then, I only had identical backup rackets with the exact same setup. This meant that if one racket was compromised by weather conditions, they all were. I had redundancy but no options.

This taught me that serious players need to think about their equipment bag the way a golfer thinks about club selection—different tools for different conditions. A racket strung tighter for hot days, perhaps a different string type for humidity, and various setups to match court speed and temperature. Equipment preparation isn't just about having backups; it's about having alternatives that can adapt to the conditions you're actually facing on match day.

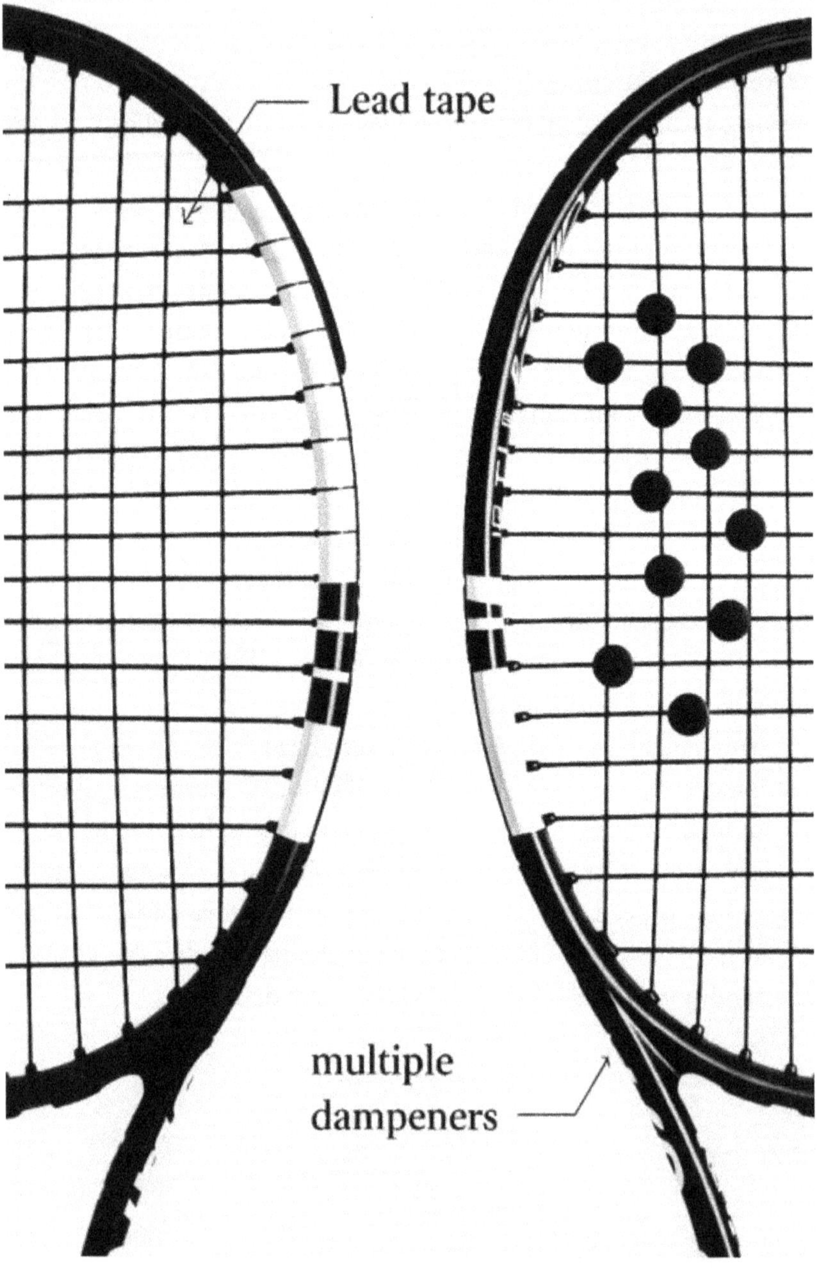
Lead tape
multiple
dampeners

35: Customize Weight

Growing up playing with wood rackets I always preferred the feel of heavier frames. Modern rackets felt too light, lacking the stability and plow-through I was used to. Knowing pros customize their frames by adding weight, I decided to do the same.

Applying lead tape at the 12, 3, and 9 o'clock positions increased weight and adjusted the balance. But I quickly discovered a problem: the lead added unwanted vibration that irritated my arm. The extra mass created harsh feedback on off-center hits, making my elbow and wrist ache during long sessions.

Looking for an alternative, I experimented with multiple vibration dampeners placed where the lead tape would go. The results surprised me—they added weight without the vibration, increasing mass while absorbing shock. It gave me the best of both worlds.

To fine-tune the setup, I used a scale to measure exact weight equivalents between dampeners and lead tape. That let me dial in precisely how much weight I was adding and where.

My current solution uses three dampeners per racket: one near the throat and two at the top of the head, secured with a rubber band so they don't fly out on mishits. It's unconventional, but it gives me the heavier feel I like without the arm problems that lead tape caused.

"The polyester revolution"

36: Spin Wins Matches

This was the most immediate improvement I ever experienced in tennis—and it wasn't just me. It helped everyone who tried it and changed the game, redefining what was strategically possible on a tennis court.

After hearing announcers praise the new polyester strings professionals were using, I decided to try them. Luxilon polyester produced even more spin than my old Gamma Rough but with better durability and consistency. The difference was instant and dramatic.

The impact of polyester strings can't be overstated: easy, repeatable spin changed tennis forever. Players from extreme angles could now flick the racket and create heavy spin, opening passing lanes and defensive shots once impossible or too risky. The margin for error grew because topspin let balls clear the net high yet still dip sharply into the court. This revolution helped shifted to baseline power and spin.

There were trade-offs. Polyester's stiffness can cause elbow issues, but I'd already learned to manage arm problems from years with the Wilson T-2000. I tested milder alternatives and hybrids—Technifibre Red Code and gut-Luxilon mixes—to reduce strain.

Still, I always returned to full Luxilon in both mains and crosses. I wouldn't give up the serve spin it produced—the ability to curve the ball dramatically into the box was irreplaceable. That serving edge alone made any minor discomfort worth it.

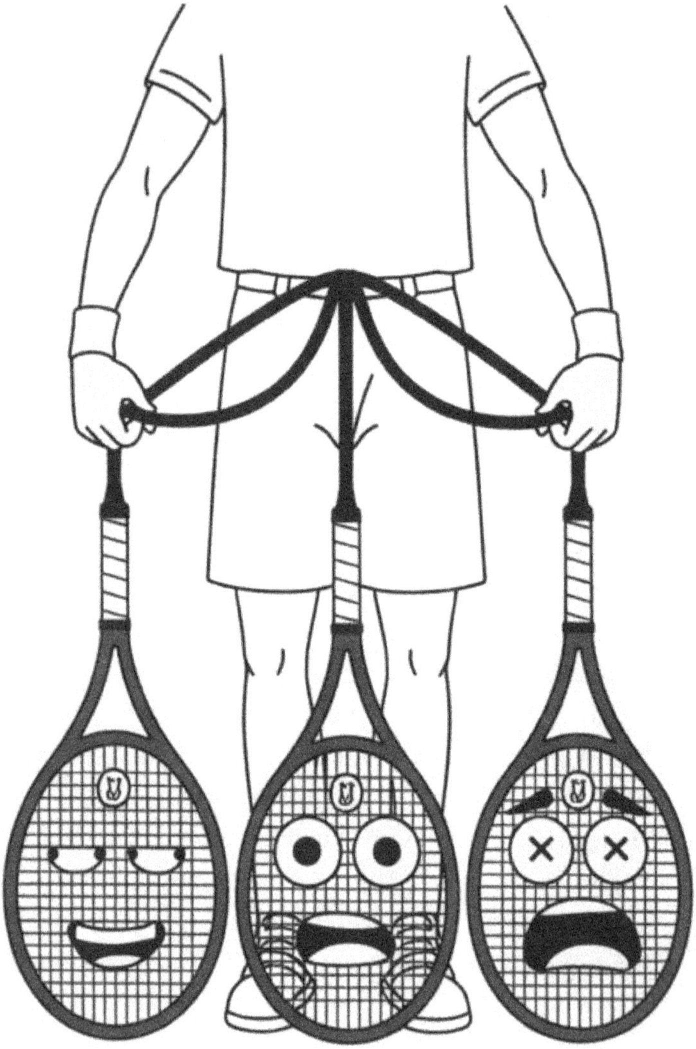

SAME FAMILY,
DIFFERENT TEMPERAMENTS.

37: New Racket, New Swing

There's an ongoing debate in tennis about equipment philosophy: some professionals play with the same racket model for their entire careers, while others constantly switch to newer technologies and brands.

My experience with Yonex rackets showed how equipment changes can demand unexpected adjustments. The sweet spot was perfectly centered, which sounded ideal but required a significant swing-path change for my passing shots. What worked with other rackets didn't translate—I had to recalibrate my technique to fit its characteristics.

Rossignol taught me another lesson: the same manufacturer and model shape doesn't mean the same performance. I assumed staying within a brand would ensure continuity, but each model had its own personality and quirks. Brand loyalty didn't guarantee a similar behavior.

The larger truth is that even "better" equipment requires adaptation. You can't just plug in new gear and expect instant results—you must adjust your game before blaming the tools. The temptation is to say, "this racket doesn't work for me," when the real issue is not yet knowing how to work with it.

Equipment matters, but the player's willingness to adapt matters more. The best gear in the world won't help if you refuse to adjust your swing, positioning, or shot selection to match what it does best. Adaptation isn't failure—it's part of mastery.

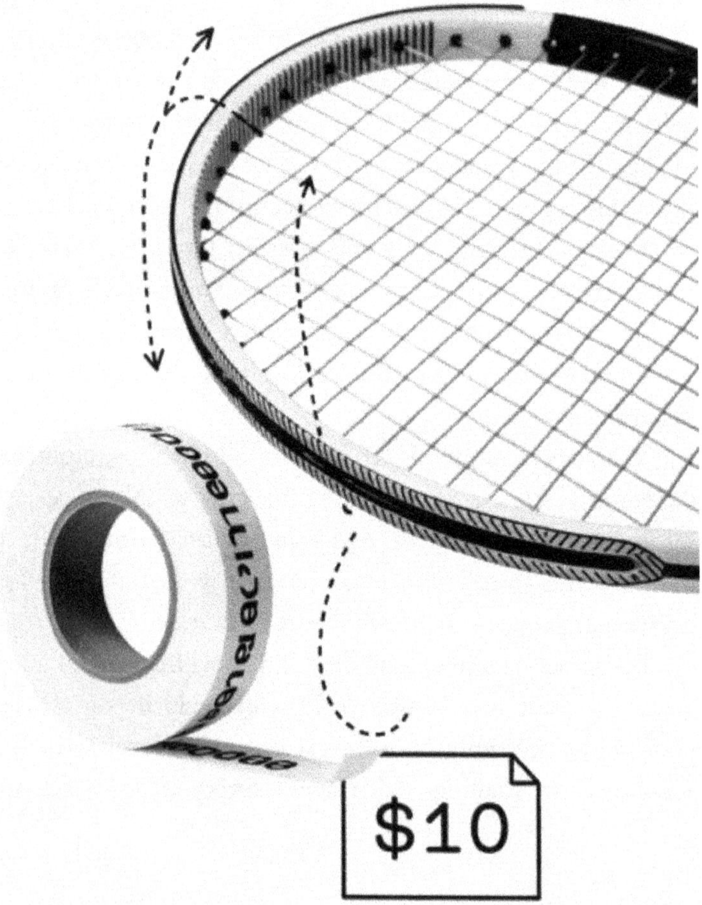
$10

38: Lead Tape: $10 Upgrade

A pack of lead tape costs less than ten dollars and can make a world of difference in performance—it's one of the best investments a tennis player can make in their equipment.

There's an important reality check about dampeners that most players don't understand: dampeners only change the sound of impact. They don't actually reduce the vibration transmitted through the frame to your arm. It's largely a placebo effect, though the altered sound can provide psychological comfort that helps some players.

The truth about lead tape is more complex and nuanced. Lead tape can either reduce or amplify vibration depending on how and where you apply it. Proper placement can enhance stability and dampen harsh feedback, while poor application can make vibration worse. It's not a one-size-fits-all solution—you need to experiment and understand what each placement does.

The bottom line is simple: customizing with lead tape is the cheapest physics lesson you'll ever buy. A few dollars' worth of lead can completely transform a racket's plow-through and stability, making it feel like a different—and often far superior—instrument. You're literally changing the mass distribution and swing weight, which are fundamental physical properties that affect every aspect of how the racket performs.

The players willing to experiment and fine-tune their setups gain advantages that have nothing to do with their stroke technique. They're optimizing the tool itself, which multiplies the effectiveness of everything else they do on court.

39: Heaviest Racket You Can Control

My wood-racket foundation taught me the value of weight early on. Playing with those heavier frames showed what mass could do for stability and power, and I carried that preference throughout my tennis life.

The physics is simple: swinging a club versus a fly swatter makes all the difference. Greater mass striking smaller mass generates more pace and stability through contact. The heavier object transfers more energy and is less affected by impact.

The problem is that most modern rackets are built very light. To make them playable for my preferences, I had to add weight through customization. It seemed backward—manufacturers were designing rackets that needed modification right out of the box.

My theory is that recreational players want to *swat* at the ball, not *swing* at it. They prefer rackets they can wave easily with minimal effort, even at the cost of losing the physics advantage of mass. The industry caters to that because it sells more rackets.

Professional wisdom still says: play with the heaviest racket you can control. That's not tradition—it's physics. But there's a speed-versus-power curve with real trade-offs. The math proves it, but the takeaway is simple: heavier is more stable and powerful until fatigue breaks timing. Find your personal tipping point through experimentation. Don't go lighter out of laziness—or heavier out of ego.

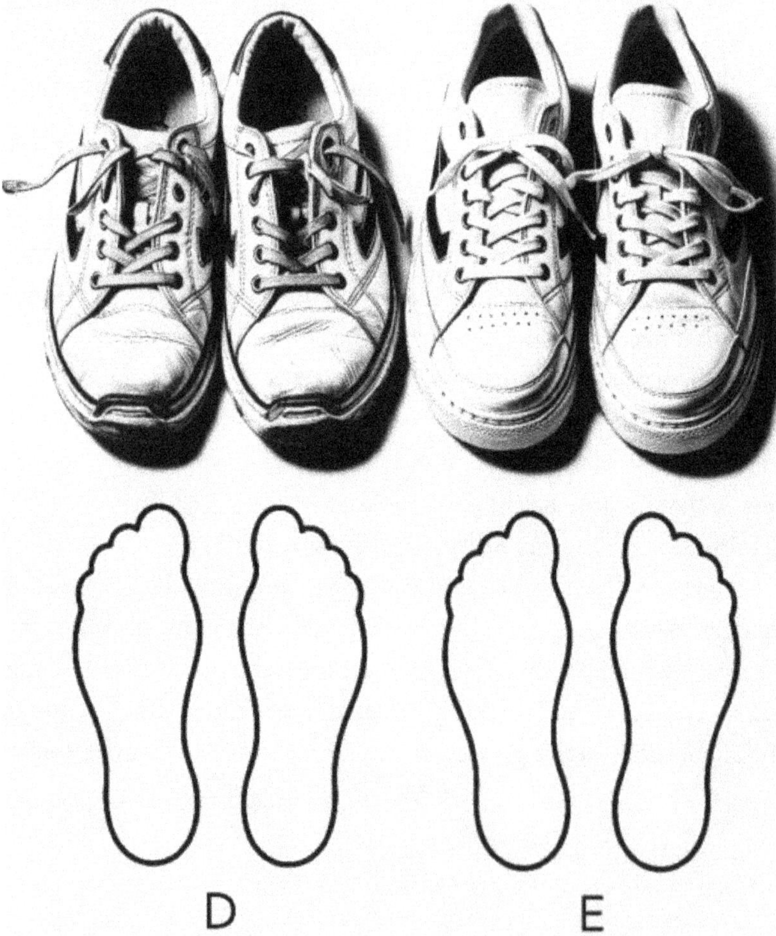
D
E

40: Shoes Matter Just Like Strings

My biggest equipment regret is not discovering wide shoes—D or E width—years earlier. The improvement in comfort, stability, and injury prevention was dramatic once I finally made the switch.

The problem is that most tennis shoes come only in standard width, with just one or two wide options per brand. Players with broad feet are forced to settle for narrow models, hoping they'll stretch or that discomfort will fade.

Once I found wide Wilson shoes that actually fit, I immediately started stockpiling. I bought four pairs in different colors, knowing what was coming—the inevitable discontinuation that plagues the shoe industry even more than racket makers.

The annual model churn is worse than in rackets. Manufacturers seem obsessed with changing or killing off models every year, making it nearly impossible to replace the perfect shoe you found twelve months ago. It's maddening for players who value consistency.

The takeaway is simple: proper width and support protect both knees and performance. When your feet are stable and comfortable, everything up the kinetic chain works better. Comfort equals confidence—you're not thinking about blisters or balance, you're just playing tennis. Start from the ground up; if your foundation is wrong, nothing else matters.

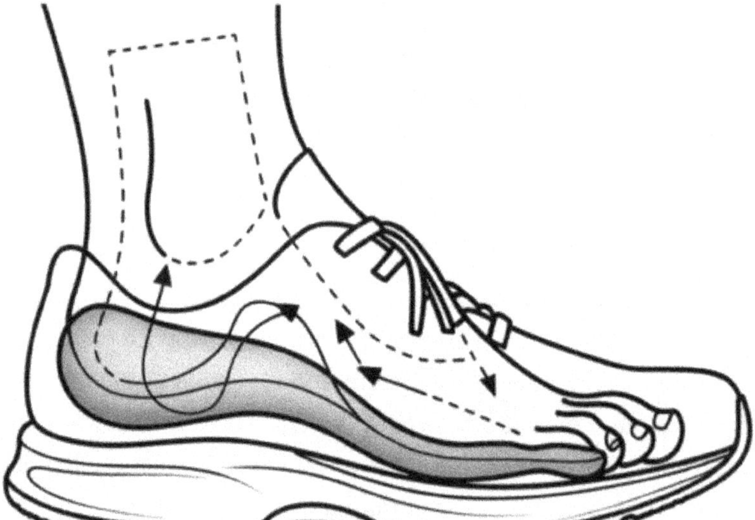

41: Orthotics Save Seasons

I faced a medical necessity when I developed plantar fasciitis and needed custom orthotics plus sonic treatment for the inflammation. The condition was debilitating and threatened to end my playing time if I didn't take it seriously.

During my experimentation phase, I tried several off-the-shelf options before discovering Birkenstock insoles with plastic over a cork base. They offered good support but created a new problem—the plastic made my wet socks slide around during play.

My arch-support revelation came with heel cushion orthotics many players recommended. They caused new issues by offering padding without real support. I learned plantar fasciitis relief isn't about cushioning the heel—it's about supporting the entire foot, especially the arch.

My current solution came from an unlikely source: the Dr. Scholl's pressure-mapping kiosk at CVS. I followed its recommendation and finally found insoles that worked for my specific needs.

The medical advice I received was clear: never walk barefoot. Even at home, wear supportive footwear to prevent aggravation. Hard-court tennis pounds the feet, and recovery requires consistent support, not just during play but all day.

Feet are equipment too. They're the foundation of your game. Well-chosen insoles let you play instead of sitting out with injuries.

AHA!

42: Find Gear that Works for You

I'll never forget picking up B. L.'s Prince Pro racket on day. Before I even hit a ball, it felt perfectly balanced—the weight distribution and swing weight just clicked. That instant connection taught me something vital about equipment fit.

Over the years, I've struggled with certain rackets, particularly thin-beam "player's frames" like the Wilson Pro Staff and Head Prestige. They simply don't generate enough pace for me. Those designs demand flawless technique and high racket-head speed, and I found myself working too hard for modest results.

I realized I needed equipment that augmented my natural stroke limitations with power assistance. Not every player has the biomechanics to generate huge pace with control-oriented frames, and there's no shame in choosing gear that fits your game rather than your ego.

That lesson hit home when a friend swore by Federer's racket, calling it perfect. I tried it, hated it instantly, and realized individuality beats imitation. Equipment should match your personality and style. Mine needed forgiveness and power help, not the surgical precision Federer's near-flawless technique required.

The bottom line is simple: your body and strokes are uniquely yours. Federer's frame won't fix your forehand, just as his shoes won't make you faster or his strings improve your serve. Use pros as data points, but find what works for *your* game, not theirs.

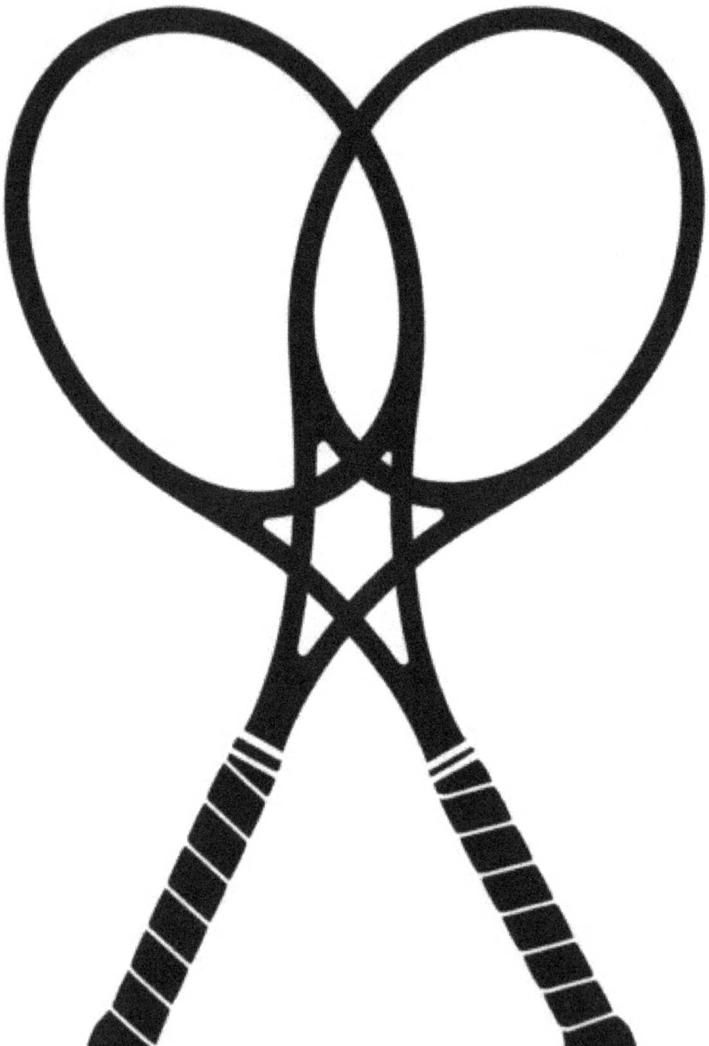

EVOLVING THE PLAYER

Improvement in tennis rarely arrives in flashes—it grows quietly through awareness, repetition, and humility. You adapt, not because your old game failed, but because the next version of you demands more. The player who keeps learning never truly ages; only the technique does.

HKRID
PROTOTYE.
SLICE
MIX

43: String = Serve

Equipment priority became clear over time: the serve trumps all other strokes when making equipment decisions. I hit more serves than any other shot in a match, so optimizing for it made sense. Everything else had to adapt to whatever the serve required.

During my string experimentation, I tried Technifibre Red Code, a softer polyester with better touch and feel than Luxilon. The trade-off was immediate—it generated less spin, especially on serves. Despite liking the improved feel on groundstrokes, I always returned to Luxilon for its serve-spin potential. The ability to curve the ball into the box and kick second serves was too valuable to sacrifice.

I experimented once with the use a dual-racket strategy—one for serving, another for returning. While intriguing, it poses a real challenge: you must still play the rest of the point with whichever racket you started. If you serve with one frame and have to volley or rally, you're stuck with your serving stick.

The logic behind serve-centric equipment is simple. You hit serves and returns in every match—those are the constants. Volleys, overheads, and passing shots depend entirely on point flow. It makes sense to optimize for the most frequent, predictable shots.

I stopped choosing strings for how they felt on groundstrokes but for the serve. Everything else had to adapt. Rather than compromising for balance, I prioritized the one shot guaranteed in every game I play.

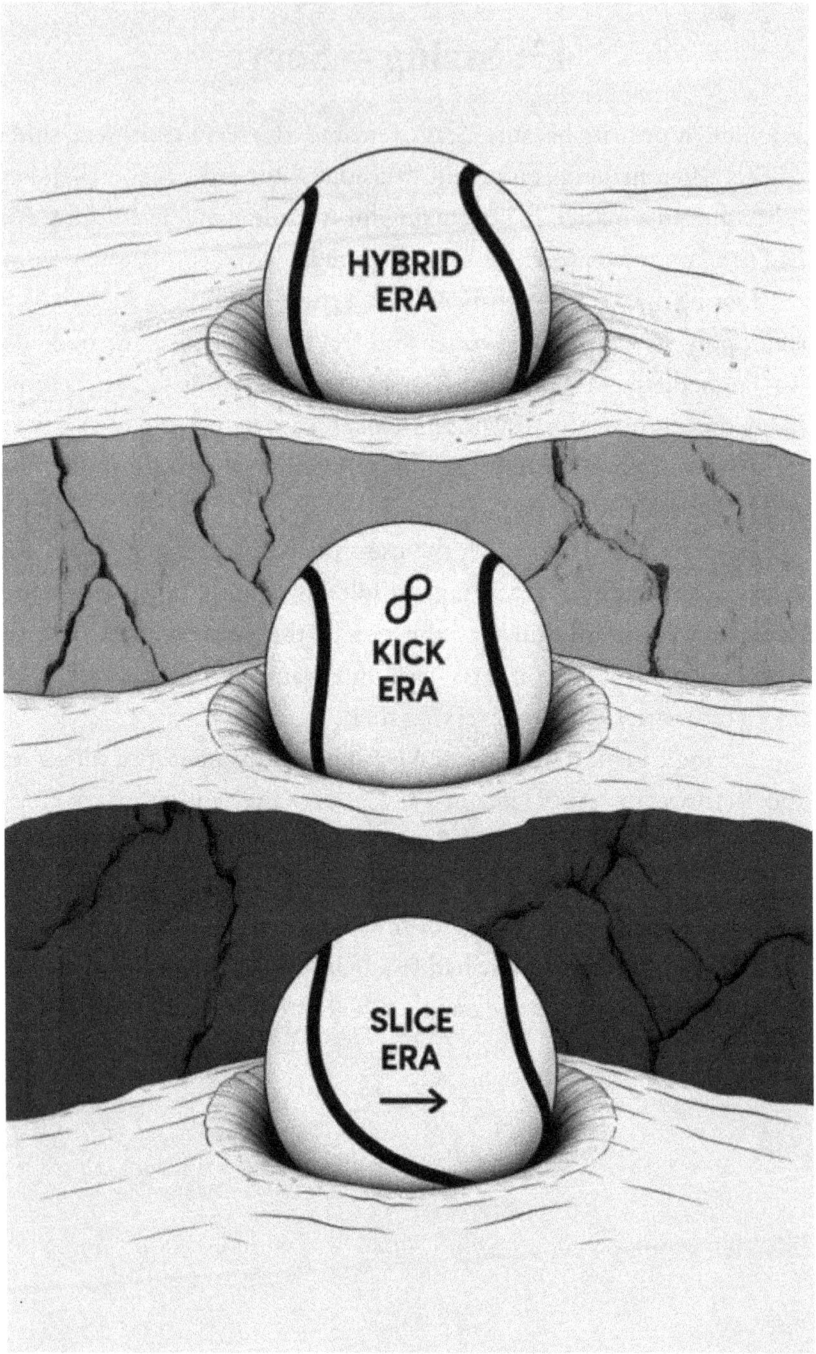
HYBRID
ERA
KICK
ERA
SLICE
ERA

44: Evolve Your Serve

My serving evolution has moved through distinct phases, each reflecting a different approach and philosophy. During my heavy slice phase, I used nearly the same motion for first and second serves, enabling a confident "two first serves" strategy. Consistency came from identical mechanics—I could aim for the same spot twice and trust the motion to repeat.

Then came my Edberg/Rafter kick phase, where everything became kick serves. The key was vertical lift through the strike zone, not horizontal drive. That prevented opponents from using my pace because the ball jumped up instead of skidding through. It was especially effective in mixed doubles. That phase ended when dusty courts killed the kick's grip.

When I first started to serve I used both arms rising together for consistency but struggled with a low toss that forced me to bend under the ball. Now I'm migrating to the toss-up and racket-arm-down sequence while fighting decades of muscle memory. Earlier service motions I lost power by keeping my shoulders level, when natural shoulder tilt provides up to forty percent of serve power.

I keep a mental library of pro motions—Murray's rhythm, Edberg's fluidity, Sinner's modern line, a relaxed delivery. These are mental cues during adjustments. Yet even as a "tennis chameleon," I can't fully reproduce certain professional motions. My serving life runs in eras—slice, kick, and now hybrid. Each phase solved the last one's weakness while creating new challenges.

45: Train Multiple Stroke Codes

I've experimented with multiple stroke variations throughout my tennis life, drawing inspiration from different professionals. McEnroe's flat touch appealed to my finesse instincts. Wawrinka's strokes showed how to generate pace through a different swing path. Modern textbook technique emphasizes getting the racket back early, using a full shoulder turn and loop momentum for power. Khachanov's full-arm topspin demonstrated yet another path to heavy rotation.

This created a practice dilemma. I split repetitions among all these variations, constantly tinkering in matches to see which worked best that day. No single style became automatic because my focus was spread across too many techniques.

Then I made an important discovery: my match performance was always far better than my practice level. Competition forged deeper muscle memory—the pressure and focus of real points ingrained movement in a way casual hitting never did. The next day I barely needed warm-up; rhythm from the match carried over.

I used to chase a single "perfect" forehand, believing one ideal technique could solve everything. Eventually I realized pros speak several dialects of the forehand language—flat drives, heavy topspin—switching instinctively with court position and opponent.

Match play decides which language fits the moment. Versatility isn't confusion—it's owning multiple tools and trusting competition to reveal which one belongs in your hand.

GO AGGRESSIVE,
PLAY SOLID
RECOVER SMART,

46: Use "Stoplight" Shot Selection

Imagine a traffic light suspended in mid-air, its color determined by where your opponent's ball lands. This simple mental framework transformed how to read the court and make split-second decisions under pressure.

Here's how it works: **Green light** means the ball has landed short, around the service line—an aggressive opportunity begging you to step in and attack. **Yellow light** signals a ball just beyond in the front half of the backcourt—time for moderate aggression, maintaining solid rally position without overcommitting. **Red light** flashes when the ball lands in the back half of the backcourt pushing you beyond the baseline into defensive territory—now's the time to play conservatively, recover your position, and reset the point.

The beauty of this system is that it uses the incoming ball's depth as an automatic shot selection cue. You're not overthinking or second-guessing yourself—the ball itself tells you what to do.

A coach once told me, "Color your decisions." Green balls demand attack. Yellow balls invite controlled rallying. Red balls require patience and recovery. It cuts through the noise instantly. Smart tennis, I've learned, is really just traffic control—knowing precisely when to go, when to slow down, and when to stop and regroup. The stoplight does the thinking for you.

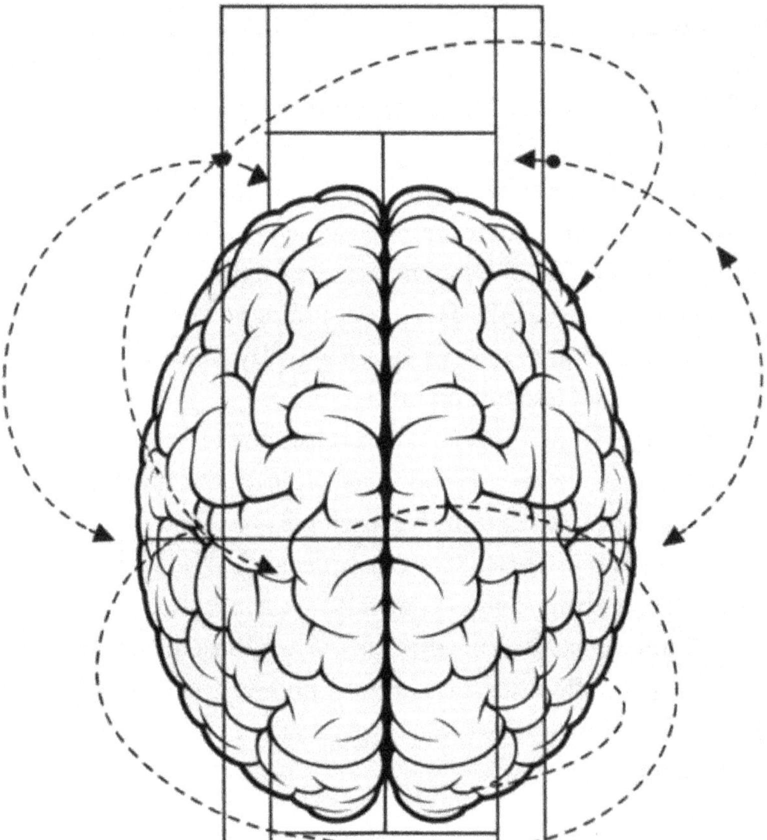

47: Study Pros, Not Just Play

A friend once asked how I became such a "cerebral player" — someone who outthinks opponents as much as outplays them. The truth? It didn't happen overnight. Like any muscle, the tactical mind develops through deliberate, sustained exercise over time.

My method was simple: I started watching other players obsessively — amateurs at local courts, pros on screen. But I didn't watch passively; I analyzed "who is doing what to whom." Where was the power shifting? Which patterns worked or failed? Every match became a lesson, regardless of level.

Tactical analysis demands mental effort, just like a tough drill demands physical effort. Yet repetition builds the skill. Over time, I connected observations into larger patterns: that backhand slice always breaks under pressure; this serve pattern creates predictable returns. Each match added another file to my strategic database.

Between sets or during breaks, I now watch others the way I once scrolled highlights—hunting for answers: who's doing what, where patterns succeed, what adjustments appear. That shift turned me from participant into analyst—and analyst into winner.

Most players miss this: practice happens even when you're leaning on the fence with a water bottle in hand. Watch with intent. Every rally is a free lesson in tactics and psychology. Cerebral players aren't born—they're built, one observed point at a time.

040

48: Serve-Volley at Pressure Points

There's a tactical weapon I carried for years but underused: serve and volley when the stakes are highest. Down 15-30 or staring at 0-40, most players—including my former self—retreat into "safe" tennis. Yet that exact moment of vulnerability is the perfect time for tactical surprise.

When the score turns against you, change tactics completely—charge the net behind your serve. You combine a shift in approach with the element of surprise, catching your opponent off-guard. They expect cautious baseline play, not sudden pressure at the net. Against equal or lesser opponents, this aggressive change often wins free points.

I had strong serve-and-volley skills but left them gathering dust, seduced by the baseline power game that defined my era. Endless rallies replaced strategic variety—a costly oversight.

Down 0-40, the "safe" play feels responsible but it's also predictable, and your opponent knows it. I once broke a losing streak by sprinting forward on the first point of every tight game. The shock alone forced two immediate unforced errors from opponents unprepared for aggression when they expected retreat.

The lesson: aggression under stress doesn't just rattle your opponent—it revives you. It pulls you out of defensive tennis and back into the fight. Surprise, I learned, is courage rediscovered. Sometimes the real risk is playing it safe.

49: Let AI Be Your Assistant Coach

A friend asked whether artificial intelligence might change how we approach tennis strategy and teaching. Curious, I ran an experiment, feeding detailed serve mechanics into an AI—toss height, contact point, radar readings tracking speed and spin. The results stunned me.

The AI didn't just offer generic advice. It produced nuanced answers citing biomechanics studies I'd never seen, connecting dots I hadn't known existed. It synthesized research into insights specific to my motion—like instant access to a team of sport scientists who'd already read everything worth reading. Feeding my serve data into AI revealed more than weeks of guesswork. It linked spin rate to toss height and confirmed what I'd felt instinctively but couldn't explain. The machine gave language and numbers to intuition.

Then came the real-world test. My wife faced an opponent using a cat-and-mouse pattern: bunting short returns to pull her forward, then lobbing over her head. We described the issue to the AI, and it suggested practical fixes—adjusting position, counter-patterns we hadn't considered. This wasn't theory anymore; AI was providing real tactical value.

Technology can't hit the ball or feel the grip, but it exposes blind spots you've ignored for years. I now treat AI as a silent hitting partner who never lies, never flatters, and never tires of questions. The future of tennis improvement is human intelligence sharpened by silicon precision. That partnership is already changing my game.

50: Apply Tilden's First-Point Rule

Bill Tilden, one of tennis's earliest legends and sharpest tacticians, claimed: lose the first point on your serve and you'll lose the game 80 percent of the time. Eighty percent—less a tendency than a death sentence hidden in one point.

When I first saw that statistic, it felt crushing, like psychological warfare disguised as analysis. Then I flipped the script. Instead of letting it haunt me, I used it as reverse-psychology fuel. If I drop the opening point—double fault, punished second serve, or a great return—I immediately double my focus on the next ball. The 80% becomes a wake-up call, not a verdict, turning panic into purpose.

Here's what I've learned: the first point shapes the narrative of the game. Win it, and momentum and confidence put you two points from safety. Lose it, and you're chasing, defending, and inviting doubt about your serve.

That's why the stat is such a powerful focusing tool. It says the stakes are real right now, not three points from now. It demands sharp concentration immediately, before you drift to 15-40.

The first point sets the story. Tilden recognized the pattern; my adjustment is to rewrite it early. Lose point one, win point two with double intensity. The game isn't over—but the fight for it has already begun.

flow state

51: Find the Flow State

I had a friend I'd play once or twice a month—solid player, consistent strokes, decent movement, but no real weapons. No big serve or killer forehand. His pace was manageable, his patterns predictable, a notch or two below my level. What I didn't realize was how much that knowledge changed my game.

When we played, I relaxed into every point. No serve to fear, no forehand bomb to defend. I wasn't worried about being pulled wide or scrambling for position. My mind stopped calculating threats; I was simply playing. And when I relaxed, something magical happened. My strokes flowed, timing felt effortless, angles opened. The ball landed where I pictured it. I played my best tennis—against the one opponent who challenged me least.

Against better players, everything changed. I was constantly managing threats—tracking serves, anticipating net rushes, covering space. My body tightened, rhythm broke. Even in victory, the flow disappeared. The lesson took years to sink in: the looseness I felt against my friend wasn't about him—it was about me. He didn't make me better; my relaxation did. The opponent wasn't the variable—my mindset was.

Now I hunt for that "calm" against anyone. Facing a big server, I remind myself they'll miss some. Seeing a weapon, I tell myself I've handled worse. I try to bring the friendliness without needing the friend—to create that psychological ease no matter the firepower.

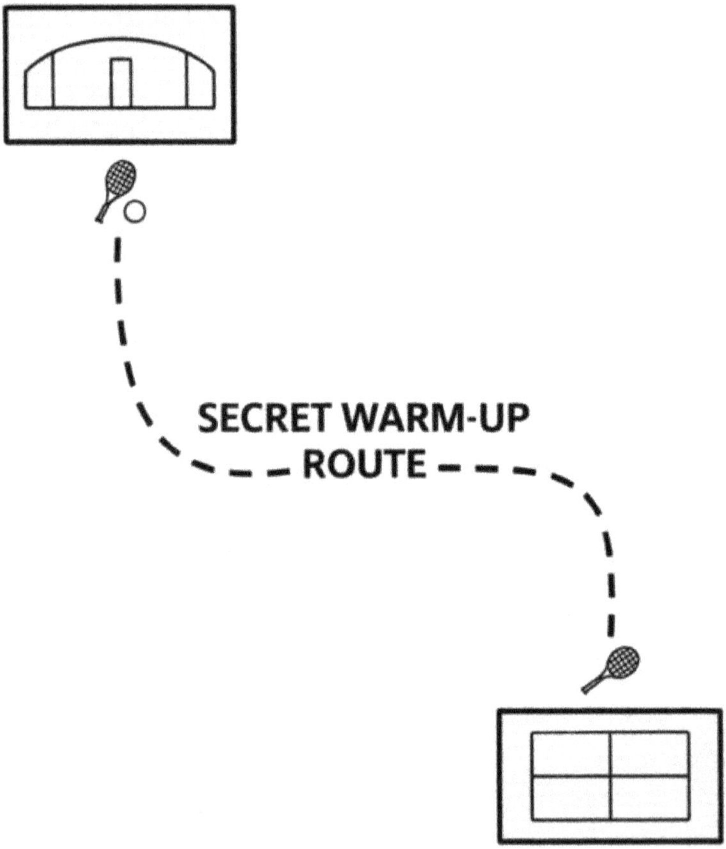
SECRET WARM-UP
ROUTE

52: Warm Up Like a Pro, Even Outdoors

The winter indoor tournament became my annual nemesis. Five minutes—that's all they gave us to warm up in that drafty facility. Cold air poured through the doors every time someone entered. Players rubbed their arms, hit a few tentative strokes, then walked on court with tight muscles and poor timing to play their match.

We would lose in the first round. Each match followed the same script: drop the first three games while my body caught up. By the time I found rhythm, we were down a set or fighting from behind.

The next year, we got creative. We found an outdoor court a few blocks away and hit there before my match. Warmed up for thirty minutes in the freezing air—serves, groundstrokes, volleys, overheads—then returned fifteen minutes before start time warmed up and ready. The tournament director wasn't amused. "You're late," he said, though we were within the default rules. As punishment, he spotted our opponents a 2-0 lead and the serve. We won because we were warmed up and they weren't.

The lesson stuck: warm muscles don't lie. You can show up on time and unprepared, or take responsibility for your readiness. Five minutes in a cold indoor court won't cut it when your opponent is giving their best. Find the outdoor court. Arrive sweating. Play ready.

53: Invest in Your Partner

We'd dominated the city mixed doubles league that spring. My partner was a ringer—strong groundstrokes, solid volleys, the complete package. When sectionals came, though, she wasn't available, and I was paired with a genuinely weak player instead. Nice woman, tried hard, but limited skills. I knew it, and the opponents would know it within three points.

Here's where I made the critical mistake: the conditions were brutal—extreme humidity—and I thought, *conserve energy*. Don't wear myself out in warmup. Save it for the points that matter. So I hit with her maybe five minutes, just enough to say we'd warmed up, then sat down conserving everything for the match.

It became a masterclass in tactical targeting. Our opponents hit every ball to my partner—returns, passes, approach. I stood there like a spectator, watching ball after ball sail past. I touched maybe ten shots the entire match that weren't returns. We lost badly. The reason was obvious once I stopped thinking about my energy and started thinking about the team: I'd left my partner unprepared.

Five minutes wasn't enough for her to find rhythm. She needed twenty, maybe thirty—to walk on court believing she could handle whatever came her way.

I'd optimized for the wrong variable. I saved my legs but lost the match. I was fresh and useless. In mixed doubles, your team's strength isn't your best shot—it's your partner's weakest shot after you've helped build it up.

54: Expect Distractions

I've played tennis in some ridiculous conditions. Once, during a high school match at a home court beside farmland, a crop duster flew so low you could smell the chemicals and feel the engine vibrate in your chest. Another time, a tournament court backed up to a freight train line. The earth shook, metal screamed, and play stopped mid-point because nobody could hear the ball or score.

But the strangest disruption was during a brutal summer tournament, I was scheduled for back-to-back matches with zero recovery time. The heat was oppressive. After finishing the first match drenched in sweat, I had maybe five minutes before heading out again. So I took off my shirt to cool down. The tournament director immediately ordered me to put it back on—dress code. Fine. For the second match, I showed up wearing a half-shirt—technically legal, but a protest against a rule that ignored dangerous heat.

I was young enough then that the temperature didn't threaten my health the way it would now. These days, I hesitate to play twice in one day, let alone in Texas summer sun. But back then, I had the resilience—and the nerve—to make a point.

What I learned from all these disruptions—crop dusters, trains, even a marching band once rehearsing next door—was that distractions only rattle you once. After the shock, noise becomes background music. The crop duster became rhythm. The train a metronome. The half-shirt, armor.

OBSERVE.
ANALYZE.
APPLY

55: Never Stop Learning

Someone once asked me how I became such a "cerebral player," as if strategic thinking were some innate gift I was born with. The truth is far less romantic: it developed over a long period, through deliberate practice, and it needs exercise like any muscle. You don't wake up one day able to read opponents and exploit patterns—you build that capacity point by point, match by match, year after year.

My practice method was simple but consistent. I watched other players constantly—amateur and pro, good and bad, singles and doubles. Between my own matches, I'd lean on the fence and study what was happening on adjacent courts. I analyzed "who is doing what to whom"—not just what shots were being hit, but why they worked or failed. I practiced observation skills when I wasn't playing, treating every opportunity as a free lesson regardless of the level of tennis being played. A 3.0 pusher could teach me something about consistency. A 5.0 hacker could show me what happens when talent lacks discipline.

Tactical analysis requires sustained mental effort, the same way physical skills require repetition. Strategic insight doesn't arrive in flashes of brilliance—it emerges from connecting discrete observations over time. Each match I watched added to my internal database: this pattern works against aggressive baseliners, that setup fails against good volleyers, this grip change signals a different serve. The knowledge accumulated slowly, almost invisibly, until one day I realized I could anticipate what would happen before it did.

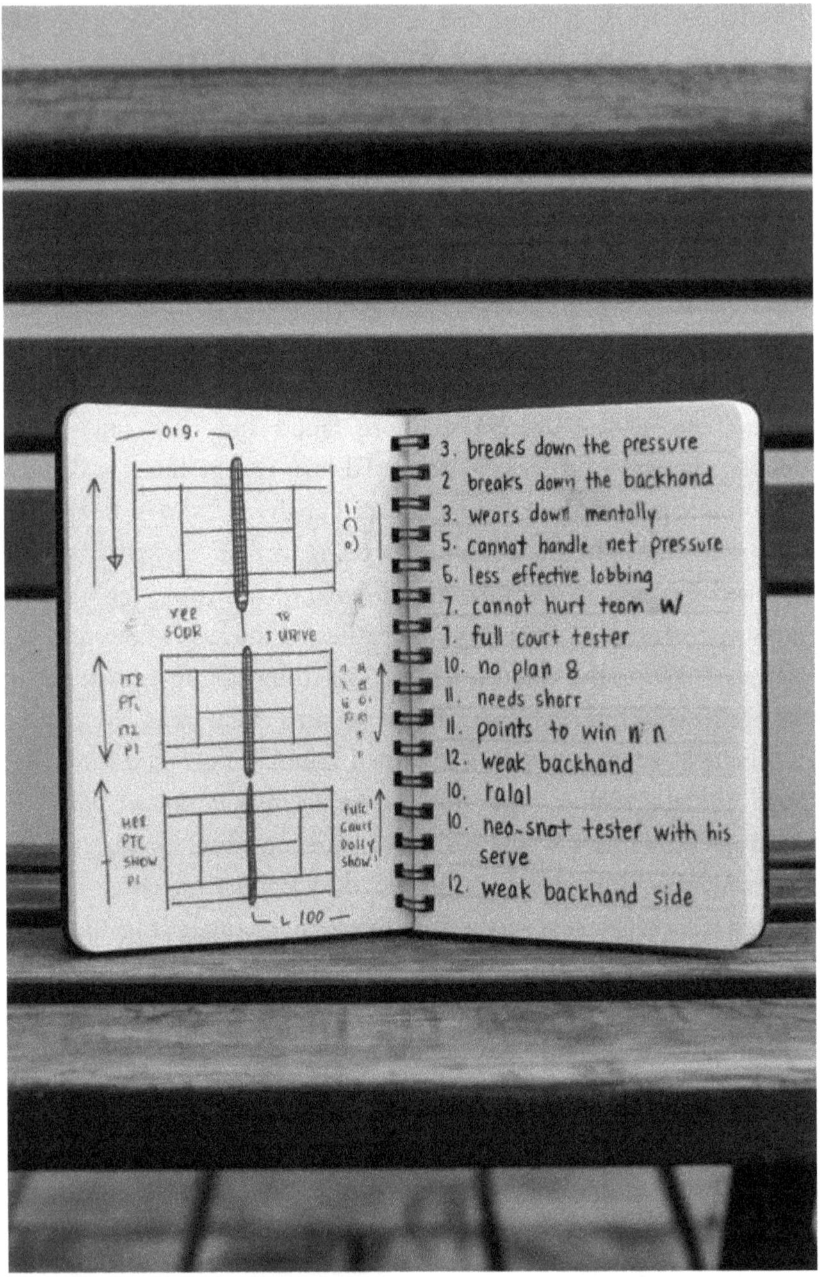
3. breaks down the pressure
2. breaks down the backhand
3. wears down mentally
5. cannot handle net pressure
6. less effective lobbing
7. cannot hurt team w/
7. full court tester
10. no plan B
11. needs short
11. points to win
12. weak backhand
10. ralal
10. neo-snot tester with his serve
12. weak backhand side

56: Enjoy the Detective Work

After decades on court, I finally understood what tennis really is: less a battle than an investigation. Every opponent arrives hiding clues in their body language, pace preferences, and shot patterns. The game stops being about overpowering someone and starts being about asking better questions. Winning then feels less like conquest and more like solving a riddle—you piece together the evidence until the answer reveals itself.

"Who is doing what to whom?" became my central question. I practiced observation skills even when I wasn't playing, treating every match I witnessed as a case study. A 3.5-level player struggling with pace could teach me as much as a touring pro dismantling an opponent. The level didn't matter; the patterns did.

So inevitably when I would play someone new for the first time it took a while to learn their game preferences and weaknesses. And this book on their game turned into a literal journal so the next time we played I didn't spend the first few games trying to remember how they played while losing points.

The shift from competitor to detective transformed how I experienced tennis. Points became puzzles. Opponents became mysteries worth solving. Curiosity replaced aggression as my primary fuel.

57: Grass: Tennis Returns to Its Roots

The smell hits you first—that distinct green scent clinging to your hands after the opening points, transferring from ball to palm with every stroke. It's an obvious detail few mention, yet it reminds you instantly that you're playing tennis the way it was first imagined.

I learned this at the Tennis Hall of Fame grass courts, on the first day, my doubles partner and I played a pristine court under clear skies. The ball stayed low and true, rewarding aggression and I found rhythm fast while my partner floundered. The next day, after overnight rain, we switched courts. Humidity transformed everything—the bounce, the speed, the feel. Now he read the surface perfectly while I misfired. Grass isn't just fast; it's alive, changing with each hour of sun and hint of moisture.

Another time the surface showed its tactical side at my friend's backyard, where three grass courts shimmered in a row. I was serving bombs until my opponent adjusted, lofting returns over my head. The low bounce that had made my serve lethal suddenly meant nothing. Yet the same slickness gave him a gift: on the ad court, he found a wide kick serve impossible on hard courts. The grass amplified its spin, skidding it beyond my reach—a shot born from the surface itself.

That's the essence of grass: it doesn't just speed the game; it transforms it. You might dominate one day and struggle the next. Every change in weather rewrites the match. On grass, the court is both collaborator and adversary—the living soul of a sport that still breathes through its oldest roots.

V1-R4 11/9/2025 12:14 PM

About the Author

D.B. Nap is an avid tennis player and science fiction enthusiast. When not hitting serves on the court, he can usually be found exploring distant galaxies through the pages of his favorite sci-fi novels. D.B. draws inspiration from the physical talents of tennis legends and the boundless imagination of great science fiction authors. He currently resides outside Dallas Texas with his wife and alien cats, patiently awaiting the invention of viable time travel. His bio photo is inspired by one of his graphic novels Dark Assassin.

Read more at RingSleepPictures.com.

www.ingramcontent.com/pod-product-compliance
Lightning Source LLC
LaVergne TN
LVHW011205080426
835508LV00007B/618
9798993046549